Overcoming Rejection

by Frank D. Hammond

Overcoming Rejection, Frank Hammond
ISBN 0-89228-105-7

Copyright © 1987, Frank Hammond
Published by **Impact Books, Inc.**
137 W. Jefferson, Kirkwood, MO 63122
ALL RIGHTS RESERVED

Scripture quotations are taken from the Authorized King James Version unless otherwise indicated.

Cover Design: David Pitts

Printed in the **United States of America**

Contents

Introduction

It is as important that inner wounds be healed as it is that physical wounds be healed. If a person receives a cut in his hand he is quick to cleanse it and protect it. Why? He knows there is the possibility of the wound becoming infected, and this would complicate his injury. This possibility of complication also applies to an inner wound. When an inner wound is experienced, it must be immediately cleansed by applying forgiveness. Forgiveness is a spiritual antiseptic. When one is wounded by rejection. He must quickly forgive the offending party otherwise, an unclean spirit (a spiritual germ) can gain entrance to the wound and cause a spiritual infection called "demonization."

Suppose that an inner wound were not cleansed by forgiveness, and that wound now becomes festered by resentment, hatred and anger. What can be done? The answer is in the cross of Jesus Christ. The substitutionary death of Jesus provides forgiveness of sin and deliverance from unclean spirits.

Jesus is the Great Physician. His atoning blood has made provision for all healing: spirit, soul and body. Jesus Himself was "wounded for our transgressions" (Isaiah 53:5), and He was "despised and rejected of men" (Isaiah 53:3).

How did Jesus react when he was wounded and rejected by others? While He was dying from the wounds of crucifixion, Jesus prayed, "Father, forgive them" (Luke 23:34). Jesus lived a sin free life. Even when rejected and crucified He did not react sinfully. Therefore, Jesus is qualified to be our Savior and Healer. "For we have not an high priest which cannot be touched with the feeling of our infirmities, but was in all points tempted like as we are, yet without sin" (Hebrews 4:15).

As Jesus was teaching in the synagogue one day, He affirmed that His ministry had been prophesied by Isaiah. "He hath sent me to heal the brokenhearted, to preach deliverance to the captives...to set at liberty them that are bruised" (Luke 4:18). Brokenheartedness is the result of inner wounding. Those who have been "bruised" need deliverance, and Jesus has come to "set at liberty" such bruised ones.

Deliverance is a healing ministry. The end result of deliverance from evil spirits is healing. The truth of healing through deliverance is set forth in several New Testament passages.

In **Acts 10:38** Jesus "healed all who were oppressed of the devil." In **Matthew 15:28** the Syrophonecian woman's daughter was "made whole" when the vexing demon went out of her. In each passage the same Greek word occurs. In Acts the Greek word is translated "healed," and in Matthew it is rendered "made whole." The Greek word in question is *iaomai* meaning "to heal, to cure, to make whole; to free from sins, errors, demons and sickness." Thus, in both contexts, the demonized were "healed" by means of deliverance.

In **Matthew 4:24** both the physically sick and the demonized were brought to Jesus, and "He **healed** them." In **Luke 8:2** mention is made of "certain women who had been **healed** of evil spirits and infirmities." In these passages, two separate

6

applications of healing are identified. Healing from the effects of demons is distinguished from physical healing. Therefore, we must ask, "What else in a person needs healing other than one's physical body?" The answer is obviously the inner man. The soul needs healing (See Psalm 41:4). One's inner man is his personality. Thus, when seven demons were cast out of Mary Magdalene, her personality was "healed."

The Greek word translated "healed" in Matthew 4:24 and Luke 8:2 is *therapeuo* which means "the care and attendance necessary to restore a person back to wholeness." Notice that the definition of "therapeuo" indicates a process of deliverance. These certain women submitted themselves to Jesus for "the care and attendance necessary" to be restored to wholeness. They were willing to do whatever He required for however long it took. They put themselves under the care of The Great Physician as one would put himself under the care of a medical doctor. Thus, these women remained under His care, accepting His diagnosis, treatment and follow up, until they were able to walk free from the power of oppressing evil spirits.

Through our Great Physician there is both diagnosis and cure. We can submit our cases to Him with confidence. There is healing: inner healing and oftentimes physical healing, for those who suffer from the wounds of rejection and their infectious complications.

> *Bless the Lord, O my soul and forget not all his benefits. Who forgiveth all thine iniquities; who healeth all thy diseases.* Psalm 103:2,3

I

Rejection: A Root Problem

WOUNDS OF REJECTION

Rejection is one of the worst, most neglected, and most common wounds. Very few persons we have counseled have not immediately identified with rejection hurts.

Rejection results from the denial of love. When one is loved, he is approved and accepted; when one is rejected he is disapproved and refused. The hurts of rejection are synonymous with refusal, denial, turn-down, rebuff, repellence, cold shoulder, slighting, shunning, spurning, ignoring, neglecting, avoiding and disapproving.

All Require Love

Each of us requires love. Love is necessary for the development of a healthy "self life." Love is to us what sunshine and water are to a growing flower. Anyone who believes that he does not require the love of others is self-deceived. The fact that all require love is clearly demonstrated by multiplied examples of what happens to the unloved. Sickness of one sort or another develops. Even pets need touching love. Dogs often quit eating, get sick, and sometimes die from a lack of love. Humane societies have been known to employ people to pet the animals to keep them healthy. What is true of dogs is also true of humans: each of us requires love, and without love we develop problems.

Rejection causes a wound to "self." When "self"

is wounded, many abnormalities can, and usually do, develop within one's personality. The wounded personality is prone to become peculiar and unstable in behavior, attitudes and opinions. Also, physical infirmities often emerge out of the emotional stress of one's rejection.

God is Love

"God is love" and His kingdom is a kingdom of love (I John 4:16). The Bible declares that God "first loved us" (I John 4:19). When God reaches out to man in redemption, He reaches out in love. "For God so loved the world that He gave His only begotten Son" (John 3:16). And, "God commendeth His love toward us in that, while we were yet sinners, Christ died for us" (Romans 5:8).

Satan Hates Love

Satan hates love. He is opposed to God, Who is Love. He wants to destroy love, for he cannot work amid love. A fish cannot survive out of water; it will soon die. Likewise, a demon cannot function in an environment that is hostile to his nature. He cannot function in an atmosphere of praise, for praise binds him (see Psalms 149); and neither can he work in an atmosphere of love, for love is contrary to the devil's nature (see John 8:42-44). Love prevents Satan from wreaking havoc in our relationships. This is why the Word of God exhorts husbands to love their wives, wives to love their husbands, parents to love their children and Christians to love one another. Love defeats the devil, but rejection opens a door of opportunity for the devil to do an evil work.

Satan builds his kingdom upon rejection. Love is nonexistent within the demonic kingdom Satan does not love the demons who do his bidding, and the demons do not love their master. Although Satan's kingdom is not divided, the unity of that

9

kingdom is not founded upon love but upon fear, control and a common propensity to evil.

TWO COMPANION ROOTS

Fear of Rejection

Once the wound of rejection is introduced into a person's life, two parallel problems begin to emerge: fear of rejection and self rejection. These two parallel problems are wrong reactions to the hurts of rejection.

When a person has been wounded, he recoils from the prospect of further wounding. The fear of additional hurt causes him to create false defense mechanisms. Whom can he trust? Will he be hurt again by the ones who have already made him suffer? Will other persons also inflict their wounds upon him? In order to prevent further hurts, he begins to suspect the intentions of others. He develops a distrust of their motives. In other words, he develops what psychologists call "paranoia." As the pattern of distrust and suspicion grows, the paranoid will eventually develop fears that others are plotting against him and become convinced within himself that others have chosen him as a target for persecution. The root behind paranoia is always "fear of rejection." The paranoid person is very tormented, and thereby the devil has gained a major objective.

Self Rejection

Further, when a person has suffered the wound of rejection he usually begins to reject himself. He may question himself, "What is it about me that repels others?" He begins to think that if he were different, or even someone else, he would be loved and accepted. After concluding that the key to enjoying acceptance by others is to become different from his actual self, the self rejected person seeks to change his personality. He may pattern his new self after a fantasy of his mind, after someone whom he has read about in a book, seen on television, or after someone whom he observes as being loved by others.

God initially made us as we are. When we reject the "self" that God has created, we open ourselves to form one or more alternate personalities, any of which will be false and demonically inspired. Thus, self-rejection is the door through which the characteristic multiple personalities of schizophrenia are enabled to enter. Such pseudo personalities are composite systems of evil spirits, representing the organizational development of the demonic kingdom within oneself.

At the time I became a pastor, I felt very insecure. I had practically no confidence in myself. When I compared myself with other ministers, I always judged myself as being less qualified and less capable than they. In an effort to improve upon my wretchedness, I would imitate other ministers whom I admired, copying, to the best of my ability, their mannerisms and personalities. One day my observant wife asked, "Why do you always preach like the last preacher whom you heard preach?" It dawned on me that I was being an imitator of others; I was not my true self.

When I was a teenager, I was tall and very slender. At six feet and two inches I weighed a mere one hundred and twenty pounds. My ears were large and stuck out from my head like the sails of a ship. My size twelve shoes looked like pontoons on my feet. My face was pitted with terrible acne sores. Who could love anyone who looked that ugly? I hated myself. I despised looking at myself in a mirror. Classmates teased me about my appearance and nicknamed me Lanky, Spider Legs, Stratosphere and Skinny. I was laughing on the outside but crying on the inside. My personal experiences with the hurts of rejection have caused me to be understanding and sympathetic toward others having battles with self-rejection.

II

Reasons for Rejection

Evil spirits are unable to enter a person at will. They must have "open doors." Rejection causes a wound, an opening, a door, through which evil spirits can enter.

After years of observation as to the sorts of things from which the average person needs deliverance, I believe that Satan forms a strategy to capture a person's life at the time of conception. Satan is unable to do all that he would like to do, for he is limited to his "legal rights." He can only take advantage of the negative conditions in one's life. For example, there may be inherited curses due to the sins of one's ancestors (see Exodus 20:4,5: Deuteronomy 30:19). The devil will perpetuate these curses to succeeding generations unless the redemptive work of Christ is appropriated through faith and deliverance (see Galatians 3:13). Too, Satan can get an opening through such things as the parents' negative attitudes and addictive habits. Now we shall see that the devil is always alert to seize the opportunities which come to him when wounds of rejection occur.

Unwanted Conception

It is common to discover that demons have entered a person when he was yet in his mother's womb. "Rejection" is an evil spirit which frequently gains prenatal entrance. A demon of rejection finds ground to enter when the parents reject their child's very conception. Why might a baby be rejected from the time of conception? For one thing, a child may be conceived in lust rather than love. The man and woman who conceive a child through fornication and adultery are seeking to indulge their sexual appetites rather than to conceive a child. An unwanted pregnancy is the result of their unrestrained lust. Few illegitimately conceived babies are wanted and loved. The child is rejected at life's beginning.

In addition to the wound of rejection, illegitimacy also produces a "bastard" curse. Under the Old Testament law, an illegitimate person and his descendants were forbidden to enter the temple for ten generations (see Deuteronomy 23:2). There are families and entire races of people under the power of illegitimate curses because of babies conceived out of wedlock.

Babies ought to be conceived in love. During her months of pregnancy, a woman can minister spiritually to her unborn infant. She can sing to him, pray for him and communicate her love. John the Baptist was filled with the Holy Spirit from the womb. A baby in the womb is capable of sensing both positive and negative spiritual influences. Some obstetricians believe that a baby knows whether or not he is loved by the time he is a few weeks formed in the mother's womb. Through my experience in deliverance, I know this is true.

Other Prenatal Rejections

Some babies are rejected while yet in the womb for such reasons as:
1. Conceived too soon after marriage. The

newlyweds plan to wait awhile before starting their family. The baby becomes an intrusion in the parent's plans and is rejected. Another example of the reasons for prenatal rejection is that of the virtuous young woman who becomes pregnant while on her honeymoon. The bride begins to worry, "what if the baby comes a little premature, who will believe that I was not already pregnant before I married? My chastity will be questioned." Thus, the woman's concern over being accused of premarital sex causes her to reject the baby.

2. Conceived too close to the birth of a previous child. The mother-to-be groans under the realization that she will be caring for two babies in diapers at the same time. She had planned to space the births of her children further apart. The baby is, therefore, rejected because its birth is deemed untimely.

3. Financial strain on the family is created. The baby comes as an "accident" and is blamed for putting stress on an already strained family budget. At today's hospital cost, birthing children is quite expensive. Some couples feel that they cannot afford to have a baby, or that they cannot afford a baby yet.

4. Fears. The mother-to-be may entertain a fear of the pain accompanying childbirth, fear of complications of pregnancy or fears of the deformity of her child. Such fears may make her wish that she had never become pregnant, which amount to a rejection of her baby.

5. Conflict between parents. The marriage may be on the verge of divorce, and it is no time to be having a baby.

6. The parents-to-be already have all the children they had planned. For example, a couple who has determined that three children will be

14

their limit, are now faced with a fourth child on the way.

7. Contemplated or attempted abortion. What happens to a baby when his rejection is so pronounced that the parents consider murdering him through abortion? There is mounting evidence that the baby is aware that his life is threatened.[1] Although the abortion is not actually carried out or is not successful. the desire to kill him is registered in the child's awareness. As such a child matures, it is not unusual for him to manifest a strong fear of being harmed or murdered by his own mother.[2]

Contemplated abortion may represent a temporary rejection of the baby. After the matter of abortion has been thought through or prayed through, eventually the child may be accepted and loved. However, the initial wound would have already occurred, and evil spirits will have taken advantage of the opening.

Wrong Sex Preference

A child may be very much wanted until he is born. As is often the case, parents desire a boy and have a girl, or they desire a girl and have a boy. The sex preference of a child is a serious matter with some parents. Nevertheless, no matter how strong the personal preference may be, it is foolish to reject a child for something that was predetermined by God and for which the child had no power to change.

In some cases one or both parents are sure that the Lord has revealed to them in advance that the

[1]See the film "The Silent Scream" for medical and visual confirmation.

[2]See *Ministering To Abortions Aftermath* by Bill and Sue Banks, Impact Books, 137 W. Jefferson. Kirkwood, Mo. 63122.

child will be either male or female. For God to reveal the sex of a child in advance of his birth is not without scriptural precedent. Both Elizabeth, the mother of John the Baptist, and Mary, the mother of Jesus, were told that they would conceive and that sons would be born to them (see Luke 1:13, 35). However, we must admit that these were exceptional cases, and for God to reveal the sex of a child in advance of its birth is not a common revelation.

An evangelist and his wife were expecting their first child. As they traveled from place to place, several prophecies were given that their forthcoming child would be a son and grow up to be a mighty servant of the Lord. Some of these prophecies were given by prominent ministers. However, the child was a girl. The father of the little girl was so hurt and confused that he seriously rejected his baby. The mother fell into deep guilt, somehow blaming herself that she had failed her husband. The infant, sensing rejection, cried incessantly and refused to let the father hold her. After my wife and I had counseled with this couple and had ministered deliverance to their precious baby, there was an instant and miraculous change. The baby became settled in her emotions and accepted her father. As they traveled on to other places, the evangelist called us several times to give updated reports that all was well and to thank us for our ministry to their baby girl.

Again, there is an illustration from my own life. My mother was expecting a girl, and it seemed very logical to her. She already had one child, a son, and she was ready for a daughter. Too, mother came from a family of four daughters and no sons. She felt she knew how to relate to girls better than boys, and she personally wanted a daughter as a companion. Before I was born, my mother had chosen a girl's name for me, but no boy's name was decided upon as an alternate. As soon as she saw me, she knew she could not name me Nellie Katherine! It was ten days after my birth before I was given a name. As I was growing up, mother often reminded me that I was a disappointment to her. Her disappointment over my not being a girl caused me to feel rejected. I could not help it that I was born a male. I could not change my gender.

In defense of my mother, I must say that she would not have knowingly done anything to harm me. She was a good Christian woman who walked in the light that she had. Similarly, there are many parents who are deeply disappointed in the sex of children born to them. The rejection of these babies is not done maliciously but out of a lack of understanding as to the consequences. Nevertheless, the wound of rejection occurs, **and the devil takes advantage of it.**

Parental rejection due to the wrong sex preference sometimes causes boys to become effeminate and girls to become masculine. A child who is rejected because he is the "wrong" sex will sense, at a very early age, that parental acceptance is gained through performing like one of the opposite sex. Consequently, a child who is rejected because of his "wrong" sex may come to hate and reject himself. Rejection of one's own sexuality can ultimately lead that person into homosexuality.

Physical Problems

A baby may be rejected at birth because he is born with misshapen physical features or outright deformities, such as mongolism. Some babies are born with cleft palates, birthmarks and various degrees of disfigurement. Not all babies with deformities and disfigurements are rejected; nevertheless, some infants are rejected, even when their deformities are slight.

Victim of Circumstance

The time of birth is an especially sensitive time. The baby is emerging from the warm, cozy environment of the mother's body. The womb has been a secure home for nine months. Now there comes an abrupt and complete change as life outside the womb begins.

Sometimes a mother is not permitted to see her baby for hours after his birth. He is taken to the hospital nursery and cared for by others. The father is only allowed to view his newborn through the glass of the nursery window. Encouragingly, changes for the better in birthing procedures have been taking place in recent years. Fathers-to-be are encouraged to attend special classes which prepare them to be present and to be of assistance when their children are born. Most of all it is important for both father and mother to hold the newborn, massage the vernix into the skin and bond to the baby. Studies indicate that children who receive touching love from the moment of birth develop more stable personalities than those who are separated from the parents at this strategic time.

The wound of rejection can occur if, for any reason, the child is deprived of a close relationship with the parents. For instance, rejection may come to a child as the result of the child being left with others while the mother is at work outside the home. The mother will pick up her toddler at the baby sitter's or child care center in time to put him to bed, and then take him back to the child care facility before he is well awake the next morning. Too, the father may work long hours away from home and may not be able to have quality time with his child. In other words, if the parents devote too little time to their child, the child will usually sense rejection from the mother and father. Proper parenting is a full time job.

Furthermore, some children are given up for adoption. This abandonment by the parents produces a severe wound. Although adopted children are usually well loved by the adopting parents, most of them are unable to receive love or to return love adequately because the wound of rejection has already occurred.

The death of one or both parents also creates a severe wound in a young child's personality. The orphaned child cannot comprehend what has happened to his parent(s) and relates to their disappearance from his life as abandonment.

Divorce is another disruptive force in the life of a child. The wound may be deepened if the little one has been subjected to an atmosphere of strife and conflict in the home prior to the divorce. Infants and little children do not have the mental capability to comprehend family upheavals, but they are able to perceive danger to themselves through the emotional environment created by conflict in the family.

An older sibling in a growing family is often forced to compete with a younger brother or sister for parental attention. The new rival may be looked upon with jealousy. Someone else on mother's lap may add up in a young mind to "mother loves baby instead of me."

Victim of Abuse

It is a well publicized fact that a high percentage of the inmates in American prisons were abused children. A survey taken in one of our federal prisons showed that **one hundred percent** of the men had been abused in childhood. This statistic reflects the dreadful consequences of abusive treatment during the formative years of a person's life. This being the case, we must learn to deal with causes rather than effects.

1. Verbal Abuse: Some children seldom hear a kind or encouraging word. They are berated, ridiculed, cursed and teased. All that some children can remember their parents saying is, "I wish you had never been born. You can't do anything right. You'll never amount to anything. You are stupid. I wish you were dead." Some children struggle even when given the best of encouragement. Who can measure the injury that occurs to children who are continually abused with cruel words?

2. Physical Abuse: There IS such a thing as child abuse, and no actual child abuse is to be defended on any grounds. However, there is a trend today to label certain forms of child discipline as "child abuse" which are NOT child abuse. For instance, some government agencies are contending that corporal punishment is "child abuse." However, a good spanking, properly administered, is scriptural and profitable. It is not abuse. It is love (see Proverbs 13:24; 29:15; Hebrews 12:5-11).

Years ago my wife and I took an eighteen year old boy into our home as a foster son. He had been taken away from his family at age fourteen due to extreme physical abuse. The emotional repercussions were so severe that he had been placed in the county psychiatric facility for treatment. This is where we found him. The authorities showed us newspaper clippings which reported the abuse he had experienced. According to the articles, his skull had been fractured in several places from being beaten with an iron rod, one eye ball had been knocked out of its socket and left dangling on his cheek, his hand had burns from being held over a gas flame and there were scars on his arms from having been burned with cigarettes. Thus, we can testify from first hand experience the toll that such abuse has upon one's personality, and we also know the restoration that results from deliverance and love.

3. Sexual Abuse: One out of every four females, and one out of every eight males, is a victim of sexual abuse. I am talking about fondling, sodomy, incest and rape. Sexual abuse creates extreme instability of personality in its victims. These wounds are usually suppressed and buried deep inside. The reason for this suppression is clear. Most sexual abuse is inflicted by close family members and friends of the family. In order to cover up the shame that might be brought upon a family, the matter is hushed, or the abused child is silenced by threats of reprisal if he exposes the offender. Nevertheless, the effects will surface in one way or another.

The devil is working overtime to bring more and more harm to children. In Sweden incest has now been legalized, and there is a push to have it legalized in other countries—even in the United States of America!

What sort of repercussions can be expected to emerge in those who have been sexually abused? My wife and I have ministered deliverance to many sexually abused women who manifested a strong hatred of men, fear of men and distrust of men.

Married women were found unable to enjoy their husbands, not because the husbands had done their wives harm, but because of a carry over of negative feelings and attitudes toward men resulting from sexual abuse in childhood. Also, demons of sexual lust and harlotry have been found to have gained entrance through sexual molestation by fathers, grandfathers, uncles and brothers. Most prostitutes have been found to be victims of sexual abuse in childhood.

In practically every case, the sexually abused experience a deep sense of guilt and defilement. The burden of shame can be crushing.

The Holy Spirit often gives us supernatural words of knowledge which bring to light the hidden roots of sexual abuse. In other instances, those being counseled have shared with us happenings in life which they have not dared to shared with any other person. We proclaim to all the Good News that there is deliverance for those who suffer in their personalities and bodies the effects of sexual abuse.

Peer Rejection

Most of us make a special effort to create a good impression on those within our peer group. We want to be accepted and not rejected. Let us not forget that we can be the offending party. We can hurt others by our rejection of them. If someone in our peer group is being rejected, we should support them rather than side with the offenders.

At one time I was part of a ministerial fellowship. At our meetings there was one brother who was continually made fun of by several others. Before long, I found myself siding in with the others. We made our brother in the Lord the butt of our jokes and jabs. We may have thought it good sport, but I sensed that our fellow pastor was being wounded by our remarks. I asked his forgiveness and thereafter made it my purpose to treat him as I wanted to be treated.

Peer rejection may occur at any time in our lives. Childhood is a vulnerable time. Children can be very cruel to one another. Strong memories of rejection often go back to school day experiences—a child laughed at and excluded from relationships because of race, manner of dress, physical appearance, social status of his family, physical or mental handicap, or even because of what his mother put in his school lunch. Children are wounded when they are not accepted by their peers.

Marriage Rejection

Separation and divorce always cause wounds of rejection. Those whom God has joined together cannot be taken apart without a tearing. Some of the worst trauma rejections come through hurts associated with divorce. The unfaithfulness of a marriage partner means that he has rejected his own for another. When the marriage covenant is broken by unfaithfulness, the hurt is the betrayal of love. When one spouse within a marriage walks out on the other, it constitutes abandonment of love.

Also, there are some spouses who live in perpetual rejection within marriage. There is no communication, no friendship and no love. One common type of marital rejection is sexual rejection. The husband or wife refuses conjugal rights to his or her spouse.

The husband should fulfill his marital duty to his wife, and likewise the wife to her husband. The wife's body does not belong to her alone but also to her husband. In the same way, the husband's body does not belong to him alone but also to his wife. Do not deprive each other except by mutual consent and for a time, so that you may devote yourselves to prayer. Then come together again so that Satan will not tempt you because of your lack of self-control. (I Corinthians 7:3-6, NIV)

Children are the innocent victims of divorced parents. They, too, may suffer deep rejection hurts by losing a close relationship with one of their parents. It is not unusual for the child of divorced parents to feel that he is to blame for the divorce or that he could have done something to prevent it. If so, he may need deliverance from guilt.

Church Related Rejection

If any two persons or group of persons ought to love one another, it should be fellow Christians. "In this the children of God are manifest, and the children of the devil: whosoever doeth not righteousness is not of God, neither he that loveth not his brother" (I John 3:10). Nevertheless, many Christians have been wounded by their own pastors, and pastors have been hurt by their people. Church members often "bite and devour" one another, Galatians 5:15. "My brethren, these things ought not so to be" (James 3:10).

Christ has commanded us to love one another. "This is my commandment, That ye love one another, as I have loved you" (John 15:12). It is a challenge to our obedience towards God to love one another. Those whom we find most difficult to love are those who need our love the most. The reason others seem unlovable is usually because they

24

have already been hurt, and they are reacting to those hurts. They are suffering in their personalities the wounds of rejection. They need others who will love them with a God kind of love. Each additional rejection intensifies the wounds of previous rejections.

III

Reactions to Rejection

When rejection occurs, some sort of reaction or response is required. Forgiveness of the offending party is the only scriptural response acceptable to God. God has commanded us to forgive others their trespasses.

> *And when ye stand praying, forgive, if ye have ought against any: that your Father also which is in heaven may forgive your trespasses.* Mark 11:25

Forgiveness is a manifestation of love. God's forgiveness of our sins is based upon His love rather than upon our merit (see Romans 5:8). God has no law against forgiving others, and expressed forgiveness slams shut the devil's door of opportunity.

Even though the trespass against us be severe, repeated and totally unjustified, forgiveness is still the only response that God will accept. If forgiveness is withheld, **or even postponed**, it gives an opening for the devil to get in.

> *Be ye angry, and sin not: let not the sun go down on your wrath: Neither give place to the devil....Let all bitterness, and wrath, and clamour, and evil speaking, be put away from you, with all malice: And be ye kind one to another, tender-hearted, forgiving one another, even as God for Christ's sake hath forgiven you.* Ephesians 4:26,27,31,32

Anyone who exercises love's forgiveness is a child of God.

> *Ye have heard that it hath been said, Thou shalt love thy neighbour, and hate thine enemy. But I say unto you, Love your enemies, bless them that hate you, and pray for them which despitefully use you and persecute you: THAT YE MAY BE THE CHILDREN OF YOUR FATHER WHICH IS IN HEAVEN.* Matthew 5:43-45a (emphasis added)

Anyone who does not show love, including love's forgiveness, is a child of the devil.

> *In this the children of God are manifest, and the children of the devil whosoever doeth not righteousness is not of God, neither he that loveth not his brother.* I John 3:10

But we may ask, "What about little children? What can an infant or a toddler do to keep out the demons of rejection? Children are especially vulnerable to the wounds of rejection. Can little children be expected to forgive those who trespass against them?"

Babies in their embryonic state are obviously incapable of exercising forgiveness toward parents or others who reject them. Since infants and small children are unable to protect themselves from demonic attack, God has appointed the parents as guardians. Most parents are careful to protect their children from physical danger. Harmful objects and substances are kept out of reach, and the little ones are not allowed to play in the street. At the same time, parents who zealously guard their children from physical harm may fail to provide spiritual protection. Parents who are outside of Christ and His truth lack the spiritual resources of authority and godly wisdom needed to protect their children spiritually. Satan is quick to capitalize on all parental neglects and failures which leave the children vulnerable.

Satan will seize upon every sinful reaction to the hurts of rejection, and evil spirits will enter that person. The demons will **link themselves together to form a demonic chain of oppression.** As more and more demons become linked together in a person's life, the degree of his bondage is increased.

Since wrong reactions to rejection open doors to demons, it is important that we learn to identify those doors and to keep them closed.

Some wrong reactions to rejection cause us to lash out at others in confrontations of anger, bitterness and rebellion. Other of our reactions, such as self pity, insecurity, fears and discouragement, are buried deep inside. The following list of wrong reactions to the wounds of rejection should help each of us identify our wrong reactions to suffered wrongs.

Rebellion

It was during the height of the hippie movement in the late 1960's and early 1970's when my wife, Ida Mae, and I were learning the ministry of deliverance. The Lord opened a special door for us to present the Gospel to hippies. In fact, we had so many hippies coming and going from our residence that the townspeople referred to me as "The Hippie Preacher." The hippies were characteristically rebellious. They opposed every valid authority. As we stripped away a hippie's veneer of rebellion, it was interesting to discover that beneath his hatred of authority was the wound of rejection. **Rejection was always found to be the root of rebellion.** These young men and women were not loved. Most of them had been seriously rejected by their own parents. Some of the hippies we met complained that their parents did not love them enough to discipline them. Their misbehavior as children had gone uncorrected. Therefore, the hippie attitude toward all authority became "If they don't love us, why should we respect them?"

Love for those in authority over us will manifest itself through submission to that authority. Jesus said to His followers. "If ye love me, keep my commandments" (John 14:15). When those in leadership either use their authority abusively or fail to function, it is easy for us to lose respect and become disobedient. Rebellion is never excused, for behind rebellion is the spirit of antichrist.

Rebellion, rooted in rejection. will produce a demonic tree with branches of self-will, independence, unteachableness, unpersuadableness, stubbornness, defiance, selfishness and pride.

Rebellion is outwardly manifested in many ways. The hippies, in part, expressed their rebellion by letting their hair grow long and by refusal to bathe their bodies. Rebellion was also expressed through the use of drugs (especially marijuana), drinking alcohol and by shameless acts of fornication. The sacredness of marriage was denied as hippie boys and girls "shacked up."

The hippie culture is a clear example of rebellion, but rebellion is by no means limited to hippies. Rebellion is found in the hearts of men everywhere, from the highest to the lowest of ranks. We must understand that rebellion is a heinous sin in the sight of God. Samuel said to disobedient King Saul, "Rebellion is as the sin of witchcraft" (I Samuel 15:23). Rebellion is a sin which is in direct association with the devil, for rebellion was inaugurated by Lucifer when he sought to usurp God's throne (see Isaiah 14:12-15).

Bitterness

Follow peace with all men, and holiness, without which no man shall see the Lord. Looking diligently lest any man fail of the grace of God; lest any root of bitterness springing up trouble you, and thereby many

29

be defiled. Hebrews 12:14-15

Bitterness is an evil fruit produced **by one's unwillingness to forgive another his trespasses.** Jesus told His disciples that they must forgive all others. Unforgiveness can make no alibis before God. It is without excuse. Furthermore, unforgiveness brings a curse. Jesus taught that anyone who asked His forgiveness for their insurmountable sin debt and then refused to forgive another in the smallest of matters, would be turned over to "the tormentors" (see Matthew 18:21-35). The tormentors are demon spirits, and to be under the power of evil spirits is a curse. The only way to escape the curse brought on by unforgiveness is through repentance toward God and forgiveness of all who need forgiving.

Bitterness and unforgiveness penalize both the unforgiving and the unforgiven. "Whose soever sins ye remit, they are remitted unto them; and whose soever sins ye retain, they are retained" John 20:23. When unforgiveness prevails, two persons become entangled in an evil bondage. The unforgiven person is held unwillingly in a broken relationship, and the unforgiving one is tormented.

As the root of bitterness grows stronger, through repeated rejections and consequential "feedings upon the hurts," it produces anger, hatred, retaliation, violence and murder. A spirit of "memory recall," a companion spirit to bitterness, keeps the painful memories of past hurts alive by continually reviewing in one's mind the times and events of those hurts.

A variety of weed invades our garden. It is named the "Careless Weed." When it first appears it is among the most frail of weeds. It can be plucked up with the fingertips. But the Careless Weed grows very rapidly, and within a few days will become taller than an eight foot stalk of corn. Its tap root will have increased to an inch or more in diameter and will be set deep in the soil. The tiny seeds of the Careless Weed are multitudinous. A gardener knows that the time to deal with a Careless Weed is at the first sign of its appearance.

Each of us is a spiritual gardener, purposing to produce the fruit of the Spirit which is love, joy, peace, long-suffering, gentleness, goodness, faith, meekness and temperance (see Galatians 5:22,23; 6:8,9). Bitterness is the "Careless Weed" that would invade our garden. The sooner bitterness is dealt with the easier it is to destroy. Therefore, "Looking diligently...lest any root of bitterness springing up trouble you, and thereby many be defiled" (Hebrews 12:15).

Self Pity

Self-pity is an inward reaction to rejection. Self-pity is a form of self affliction whereby one permits himself to indulge in thoughts of unfairness until he becomes thoroughly miserable. It is a practice guaranteed to destroy joy and peace, two of the precious fruits of the Holy Spirit.

Escapism

The Psalmist, David, expressed the desire to escape from his oppressors in these words, "Oh that I had wings like a dove! for then would I fly away, and be at rest" (Psalm 55:6). Most of us know well the feeling of "just wanting to get away from it all." When the circumstances of life turn sour, it is a temptation to run away. Hurt people often become escape artists who devise clever ways of escaping the unpleasantness of life.

31

A common form of escapism is day dreaming whereby a person creates his own pleasant world and lives in that world through his imagination. He shuts out of his mind the reality of stressful circumstances and withdraws into unreality. He may be aided in his escape endeavor by movies, television dramas or fiction books.

Another route of escape is through sleep. As long as one stays in bed, hiding under the cover, he is not having to face responsibilities or unpleasant things. Therefore, sleep can become an addiction, an obsession, a futile attempt to sidestep life's problems.

Drugs and alcohol can be utilized to "bomb the mind" so that it cannot dwell on unpleasant thoughts. Tranquilizing drugs and electric shock therapy are professional techniques of inducing escape routes for mental patients. These medical techniques cure nothing and often create greater problems. God has something better.

Guilt

Guilt is the most needless burden that a person can bear. The whole purpose of God's redemptive work in Jesus Christ was designed to deliver us from sin and its consequences. Guilt is a major consequence of sin. Under the law there was no remedy for guilt (see Hebrews 9:9,10), but under the New Covenant, "There is therefore NOW no condemnation to them that are in Christ Jesus, who walk not after the flesh [works of the law] but after the Spirit" (Romans 8:1) (emphasis and amplification added). When one has sinned, there is a remedy. Through repentance of sin and faith in the Lord Jesus Christ, the blood of Jesus removes sin and its corresponding condemnation.

For if the blood of bulls and of goats, and the ashes of an heifer sprinkling the unclean, sanctifieth to the purifying of the flesh; How much more shall the blood of Christ, who through the eternal Spirit offered himself without spot to God, purge your conscience from dead works to serve the living God? Hebrews 9:14

Some people feel guilty even though they have not sinned. These poor souls do not perceive Satan's clever plan to torment men with unfounded guilt, and they unnecessarily blame themselves for the evil done to them by others. Their reasoning goes like this, "I deserve the way I am treated. My woes are all my fault. My plight is a judgment from God." In most cases these negative attitudes toward self are the end result of having been belittled and blamed by others, usually one's own family. What a hellish burden it is to think that all one's hurts are deserved and that there is no remedy!

It is quite common for others to transfer their guilt to someone else. When God confronted Adam with his sin, Adam said, "The woman whom thou gavest to be with me, she gave me of the tree, and I did eat" (Genesis 3:12). Thus Adam transferred his blame to God and his wife. Then, when God confronted Eve, she said, "The serpent beguiled me, and I did eat." Thus, Eve refused to accept responsibility for her sin and contended that the devil made her do it. God says in His Word that each of us is responsible for our own sins:

Let no man say when he is tempted, I am tempted of God; for God cannot be tempted with evil, neither tempteth he any man. But every man is tempted, when he is drawn away of his own lust and enticed. James 1:13,14

Indeed, guilt is a heavy and needless burden. If the guilt is due to one's own folly, let that sinner be plunged beneath the crimson tide that flowed from Emmanuel's veins, for thereby he is made as white as snow. If one has assumed the guilt of others, let him lay that burden down. God would have him bear the burden of intercession, but not of guilt. If one has been wrongly blamed as the cause of another's sin, let him rest upon the justice of God. "So then every one of us shall give account of himself to God. To his own master he standeth or falleth" (Romans 14:12,4).

Inferiority

Inferiority is closely related to rejection. One who is rejected, who is put down by others, is prone to put himself down. When he compares himself with others, he evaluates himself as inferior. When he takes inventory of his capabilities, he judges himself to be inadequate.

In God's sight no man is inferior. God has given each of us our own abilities and responsibilities. The parable of the talents teaches us that God has given to some more responsibility than others, and all that God requires is faithfulness in whatever is entrusted to us.

Insecurity Fears

There is security in love. When our earthly father loves us, he conveys to us an understanding of the Heavenly Father's love, and it is easy for us to believe that our Heavenly Father loves us, too. The person who knows beyond any doubt that God loves him will have stability in his life. He will declare with Paul, "If God be for us, who can be against us" (Romans 8:31). On the other hand, the person who is not loved by those who should love him is prone to doubt even God's love. The resultant insecurity produces fear. What will happen to me? Since "fear hath torment," the rejected person becomes tormented (I John 4:18). He worries over points of security pertaining to everything from finances to favor with God.

Our security rests in God's love. When we are confident that God loves us, fear is cast out.

There is no fear in love; but perfect love casteth out fear: because fear hath torment. He that feareth is not made perfect in love. I John 4:18

Hopelessness

The individual who sees no prospect of being loved is like a man trapped in a vast desert with nothing but miles of burning sand in every direction. His tongue swollen with thirst, he falls on the desert floor awaiting death. He is utterly hopeless.

The one wounded by rejection is without refreshment. He begins to dry up inside. His hopelessness leads to discouragement, despair, dejection, defeat and depression. Without hope there is no joy; without joy there is no desire to live. Agreement with death is a path which leads to heaviness of heart or possibly even to suicide.

When the hopeless finds love he finds hope. Love relationships are like wells of living water, especially our relationship with Jesus who declared, "If any man thirst, let him come unto me, and drink" (John 7:37). One who has a personal relationship with Jesus receives a well of living water inside himself. Jesus explained to the woman of Samaria, "Whosoever drinketh of the water that I shall give him shall never thirst; but the water that I shall give him shall be in him a well of water springing up into everlasting life" (John 4:14).

When we give love to another we are giving "a cup of cold water" to him in the name of Jesus. The hopeless will be refreshed by our love. On the other hand, the one who needs refreshing love from others must not sit idly waiting for others to take the initiative. Those who feel hopeless and desire to be loved should begin to pour out their own love in abundance. Christ's teaching on giving and receiving applies to love as well as to material things.

Give, and it shall be given unto you, good measure, pressed down and shaken together, and running over, shall men give into your bosom. For with the same measure that ye mete withal it shall be measured to you again. Luke 6:38

Defensiveness

If your pet dog is hurt, you will do well to touch him with caution, for he might bite you. Hurt people may "bite" you, too (see Galatians 5:15). A wounded person can be sensitive and defensive, returning not only evil for evil but also evil for good.

Defensiveness expresses itself in criticism and judgmentalism. Judgmentalism takes the position: judge others who have hurt you, and judge others who have judged you. Judgmentalism is a false protection. Instead of providing security, judgmentalism invites retaliation from others.

Judge not, that ye be not, judged. And with what measure ye mete, it shall be measured to you again. Matthew 7:1,2

Judgmentalism blinds one's own eyes to his own faults. He becomes self-deceived. He can only see the faults of others. This brings to mind the teaching of Jesus about the mote and the beam. We must first remove the beam from our own eye before we can see clearly to remove the mote from our brother's eye.

Judgmental people are also prone to project their own faults into others. A person in my congregation accused me repeatedly of not loving the people in the fellowship. His accusation caused me to fall into introspection in an effort to discover what I had said or done to convey to any one that I was deficient in love. Finally, I realized that the accusing person himself did not love others. **Instead of seeing the problem within** himself, he had transferred it to me. Afterward, I discovered that **transference of blame** is a very common deception on the part of those who suffer from the wounds of rejection.

When we have been trespassed against, it is not our responsibility to stand up for our rights and to justify ourselves. Jesus said!

> *Ye have heard that it hath been said. An eye for an eye, and a tooth for a tooth. But I say unto you, That ye resist not evil but whosoever shall smite thee on thy right cheek turn to him the other also.* Matthew 5:38,39

Neither need we tear others down in an effort to build ourselves up. God is our defense; therefore, "Be not overcome of evil, but overcome evil with good" (Romans 12:21).

Distrust and Disrespect

Trust is a bridge that unites one person with another. How can one trust and respect those who have wounded him by rejection, betrayal, abandonment or unfaithfulness? When trust has been destroyed, relationship is destroyed. Trust can be reestablished, but it can only be accomplished with great effort and with great caution. The rebuilding of trust takes time, patience and persistence.

As a plausible example of destroyed trust, consider the plight of a daughter who is rejected by her father from childhood. Her father does not take time to play with her, he drinks heavily and is abusive. When this little girl reaches adulthood she will more than likely have a strong distrust and disrespect of men in general. Whether the man in her life is her husband, pastor or any other man, her fears will tell her that all men hurt women and no man can be trusted. The torment of distrust and disrespect must be rooted out and overcome by trust in God. As one becomes secure in God's love, he will be able to endure other's injustices without suffering inward repercussions.

Distrust and disrespect can not be excused or justified. The Bible commands a child to honor his father and mother, and commands a wife to respect her husband (see Ephesians 5:33; 6:2). It is natural for those under the headship of parents and husbands to honor those who are kind, compassionate, helpful and unselfish. It is more difficult, although not impossible, to respect an authority just because God commanded it. The one who maintains respect, even though abused, finds favor with God.

If, when ye do well, and suffer for it, ye take it patiently, this is acceptable with God. I Peter 2:20

Hardness

God created turtles with protective shells, but he did not make people with shells. When a person forms his own shell of protection, he develops a "turtle personality," hard and impenetrable. He says to himself, "I don't intend to be run over and hurt by other people any longer. I am rough and tough. I will not let anyone get through to me." So, he creates a hard shell about himself, and he acts like a snapping turtle.

When other people are trying to do us harm, we

may forget that God is our Refuge and Strength, our Rock and Fortress. We may, instead, build a hard shell around ourselves and withdraw into a self constructed defense mechanism. The problem with our hardness is that it robs us of compassion. Thus, we are hindered from fulfilling our ministry to others.

> *Finally, be ye all of one mind having compassion one of another, love as brethren, be pitiful (compassionate), be courteous.* I Peter 3:8

Summary

We have reviewed some of the most common reactions to rejection. Each of these reactions represents a departure from God's counsel and constitutes sin. "Sin" doors become open invitations for demons to enter. The devil crouches at the sin door waiting for an opening to spring in and devour.

When Cain became upset over God's refusal to accept his bloodless sacrifice his heart was filled with hatred and jealousy toward Abel. God immediately warned Cain:

> *Why are you angry? And why do you look sad and dejected? If you do well, will you not be accepted? And if you do not do well, sin crouches at your door; its desire is for you, and you must master it.* Genesis 4:6,7 Amplified

There are positive, scriptural solutions to all our hurts and frustrations. We must learn not to react sinfully to suffered wrongs, but we must instead walk in the counsel of God's Word.

IV

Readjustment to Rejection

Once the wounds of rejection have occurred, efforts must be made to relieve the hurts and to find ways to satisfy the love need in one's life. He seeks to readjust to the wounds of rejection and to find ways to compensate for his hurts. The following paragraphs identify and comment on the common methods people employ in readjusting to the wounds of rejection.

Perfectionism

"How can I get love? I cannot force other people to love me. If I can only get a little approval from others, maybe that will seem like love and make me feel appreciated." So reasons many a wounded person.

People who feel unaccepted and unappreciated are prone to become perfectionists. They hope that by doing something perfectly others will say approvingly, "I think you are wonderful. How did you do that? I wish I could do that as well as you can do it."

Because of my own battles with rejection and insecurity, I became a perfectionist. It is an unrealistic undertaking to be perfect in everything, so one is forced to specialize. I specialized in scheduling and precision performance. Perfectionism is a hard taskmaster. One is required to drive himself in order to accomplish his goals. He may lose sleep and over extend himself physically, but no price for approval seems too high to pay.

In order to plan my perfect daily schedule, I would awake an hour early and think through my entire day. I would decide exactly what I would do and fit it into a time frame. Theoretically, at the end of the day I would have had a perfect day. When all would go as planned, I would be puffed up with pride, and I would think to myself, "I can plan and work a schedule better than anyone." Unfortunately, there were many interruptions and unpredictable contingencies which were not calculated into my plans. When plans went awry, there were frustrations, impatience and intolerance toward self or toward anyone who could be blamed for the failure. Anger would erupt over the most inconsequential disruption of plans.

After I became a pastor, I would plan my days carefully. My daily routine was detailed, but it left no room for unexpected emergencies in the fellowship which called for my participation. For example, if a church member went to the hospital for emergency surgery, I deemed it an unjust interruption of my perfect schedule. Their getting sick just ruined my day! **Keeping a perfect schedule became more important than the lives of the people God had called me to serve.**

Perfectionism also puts others under bondage because the perfectionist expects those around him to perform with equal dedication and skill. When this demand for perfection in others involves one's husband or wife (as it did in my case), it puts a strain on the marriage.

An example of perfectionism personified is the woman who is a perfectionist housekeeper. Even if one goes into her house at nine o'clock in the

41

morning, he will find all the dishes washed, floors vacuumed and beds made up. Everything will always be neat and clean. She will not even tolerate trash in her wastebaskets. When she is complimented for her achievements, she will be filled with pride. If altered circumstances interfere with her perfection goals, she becomes frustrated and irritable.

It is commendable to be neat and orderly, but **perfectionism is bondage.** The perfectionist is physically taxed to keep up with unrealistic and unnecessary goals of performance. He feels that perfect performance is the key to acceptance. The devil will inflict heavy burdens whenever he can, but Jesus says, "My yoke is easy, and my burden is light" (Matthew 11:30).

False Compassion and False Responsibility

The person who feels unloved can become desperate for relationships. "Isn't there someone I can love?" he ponders. Out of desperation for companionship, one is tempted to become involved in potentially dangerous relationships. For instance, a Christian man may seek out a woman who has fallen into sexual promiscuity. He convinces himself that God has called him to be her savior. He feels a compassion to help her and to witness to her of Christ, but his compassion is false. He is really seeking to fulfill his own love needs. The temptation he encounters is too great, and he falls into sexual sin.

Many marriages are headed for disaster from the start because they are founded on false compassion and false responsibility. For example, a pure, Christian woman chooses to become involved with a man who is in the depths of sin. She believes that unless she helps him no one else will, and that God will hold her responsible for his damnation. God is not requiring this responsibility of her. Through fantasy deception she convinces herself that she will be the catalyst which will turn him into an angel. She marries him in order to rescue him, but in the end she will, nine times out of ten, either follow in his ways or enter into a life of heartache and suffering.

> *God is faithful who will not suffer you to be tempted above that ye are able; but will with the temptation also make a way to escape, that ye may be able to bear it.* I Corinthians 10:13

The "way of escape" can be the avoidance of relationships based on false compassion and false responsibility.

Another facet of false compassion manifests itself through an inordinate affection for animals. Pets seldom reject their owners. A man can have a bad day at work, and all his friends turn against him, but when he comes home in the evening his dog will still love him. His dog will bark a welcome, jump up on his master, wag his tail, lick his owner's hand and roll over on the floor. All this dog-activity adds up to, "I love you; I'm glad you're home."

It is not wrong to have pets, but it is wrong to rely upon them for companionship and love. God brought all the animals He had created before Adam who named each of them, "but for Adam there was not found an help meet for him" (Genesis 2:20). No animal in all the world could complete Adam's need for companionship.

How can one judge as to whether his relationship with pets is unbalanced? First, does one humanize his pet? Does one treat his pet as though

43

it were human, a member of the family? Some pet owners refer to their little animal as "my baby," and they sign the pet's name on Christmas cards and personal letters. Again, does one dehumanize himself in order to relate to the pet on its level? Some pet lovers have taken on animal personalities through their desire to commune with that animal. In deliverance session we have seen demons manifest animal characteristics in people. The demons have sometimes caused those with inordinate affection for animals to bark like dogs, hiss like cats and neigh like horses. Yet another test for an imbalanced affection for animals is to weigh one's evaluation of animal life against that of human life. Those who have been rejected by people and accepted by pets may rather see a person injured or killed than to see an animal suffer. I have also discovered that people who have inordinate affection for animals become very defensive of their relationship with animals. It is a threat to their love security to suggest that they be required to change their love priorities.

Material Lust

The absence of love leaves a big vacuum in one's life. This vacuum will soon be filled with one thing or another. Satan is always around to offer his substitutes for love. Satan has no love to offer, so he offers lust. He may suggest lust for power, recognition, money or sex as the cure for love-emptiness. Love satisfies, but lust never satisfies. Lust always leaves a void and a greater hurt.

Then, when lust hath conceived, it bringeth forth sin: and sin, when it is finished, bringeth forth death.
James 1:15

There seems to be a certain kind of comfort experienced through obtaining resort houses, exotic automobiles, fur coats, elaborate sports equipment, lavish vacations and fine wines; but, one is still left with his inner emptiness. **The lust for things is never satisfied with whatever is obtained.** Lust's appetite demands more and more things.

Lust is a condition within the heart. There can be lust for things apart from obtaining things. Some people controlled by lust actually live in poverty and have very few earthly possessions, yet a war goes on within themselves.

> *From whence come wars and fightings among you? Come they not hence, even of your lusts that war in your members? Ye lust, and have not: ye kill, and desire to have, and cannot obtain: ye fight and war, yet ye have not, because ye ask not. Ye ask and receive not, because ye ask amiss, that ye may consume it upon your own lusts.* James 4:1-3

Material things will never substitute for love. Neither, all the money in the world nor all that money can buy, will ever fulfil one's love needs. The world advertises its wares enthusiastically and would have us believe that "things" will satisfy. Moses set an example for us when he chose God's way instead of the world's way. He had wisdom to see that the pleasures of this world are very temporary while the rewards of serving God are eternal (see Hebrews 11:24-26).

Sexual Lust

Very few persons seem to have escaped Satan's snare of sexual immorality. Why is sexual sin so prevalent even among Christians who have been taught the moral standards of God? For one thing, the world is bombarding us through the media with programs depicting fornication and perversion as acceptable mores for modern man, and multitudes have welcomed this new philosophy as "liberation." But, Satan, the god of this world, is a deceiver. What first appears as liberation is later discovered to be bondage.

Persons who have been robbed of deserved love are especially vulnerable to the temptations of sexual sins. The love hungry are deceived into thinking that their love need can be met by gratifying their sexual appetites in illicit ways.

Fantasy lust is mental indulgence in sexual sin. Such agreement with sin gives opportunity to the devil. It is a false concept to think that demons can only take advantage if there is overt sin. Lust has its start in the mind and in the eye, but the devil will push a person as far as possible into the mire of sin.

> *Ye have heard that it was said by them of old time, Thou shalt not commit adultery: But I say unto you, That whosoever looketh on a woman to lust after her hath committed adultery with her already in his heart.*
> Matthew 6:27,28

Mental acceptance of the devil's lies opens the door to acts of sexual sin. Masturbation is one of the earliest expressions of sexual violation. Masturbation is a form of self love. It is often fostered by pornographic materials. Those who feed their eyes and minds on pornography open themselves to every sort of perverse spirit. The thought life becomes polluted and the conscience becomes seared. All that is needed is an opportunity to practice what has been enjoyed in the imagination.

No matter how far an individual pursues the path of illicit sexual indulgence, whether with another of the opposite sex or another of the same sex, he will never find the rainbow of fulfillment. Instead, he will reap exactly as he has sown.

*And the men also turned from natural relations with women and were set ablaze (burned out, consumed) with lust for one another, men committing shameful acts with men and **suffering in their own bodies and personalities the inevitable consequences and penalty of their wrong doing and going astray,** which was (their) fitting retribution.* Romans 1:27, Amplified (emphasis added)

Self Promotion

There is an old adage which says, "Two wrongs do not make a right." **It is equally true that "Two opposite problems do not make a solution."** It is a blatant deception from the enemy that offers relief from one problem by giving us the opposite problem. Suppose I have a severe headache, and someone offers help. His way of help is to stomp on my toe so hard that it will take my attention away from my head. That is the kind of help the devil offers. He says, "You poor thing. You are hurting so much from rejection. What you need is an ego trip. Build yourself up in your own estimation until you feel good about yourself." When this proposition from the devil is translated into truth it really says, "Since you have a bad relationship with another person, it will help you to have a bad relationship with God." Pride puts us in trouble with God who says, "Everyone that exalteth himself shall be abased" (Luke 18:14). Compounding the problem does not create a solution.

Suppression

Most of us are experts at fooling ourselves. For instance, we think we have genuinely solved a problem because we do not let it worry us any longer. If we have cast every care upon the Lord, then well and good; however, if we have merely suppressed the problem, it will eventually surface again. Faith in God is a cure, but suppression is a psychological trick.

Suppression is defined as "exclusion from consciousness." This can be achieved by a technique of the mind, or it can be induced by other means. For example, a few tranquilizing pills, a bottle of bourbon or electrical shock treatments will exclude from consciousness practically everything in one's mind, but one's problems will remain unsolved.

It is beyond dispute that many physical ailments are due to suppressed resentments, fears, worries, anxieties and guilt. The prayer lines in Pentecostal churches are choked with chronic cases of peptic ulcers, diverticulitis, tension headaches, heart palpitations, arthritis and stress cancer. Such diseases are often the result of suppressed emotions. The root cause of these physical ailments needs to be eliminated before genuine healing can take place.

Do not be wise in your own eyes, fear the Lord and shun evil. This will bring health to your body and nourishment to your bones. Proverbs 3:7-8, New International Version

Attention-Getting Devices

People who feel ignored and inferior will often develop bizarre behavior to attract attention. Children who are neglected by their parents will often misbehave. Even if the unruly child gets a spanking at least he is getting attention.

A young man was recognized in his peer group as "the life of the party." Nothing ever seemed serious to this boy. He was forever telling jokes and making quips. He thoroughly enjoyed the attention he received from his constant antics. When this young man was twenty five years of age, the Lord called him to be a minister, but he felt so inadequate and inferior that he resisted the call of God with all his might. His mother noticed that he was acting very somber, and she was concerned that something was seriously wrong with him. The mother confronted her son with, "You are not acting normal. What is the matter with you?" The young man was reluctant to admit to his mother what was going on inside himself, but she kept pressuring him until he told her the truth. He said that God was calling him into the ministry. This Christian mother, who had often prayed that God would call at least one of her three sons into the ministry, said to this son, "I don't believe it! You are twenty five years old, but as far as I know you have never had a serious thought in your head." This was the mother's opinion of her grown son. I am that son.

My foolishness was a cover up for my insecurity and inferiority. I was laughing on the outside, but I was crying on the inside. A lot of people are like that. They become amateur clowns, daredevils and religious extroverts in order to draw attention from others.

Control Of Others

There was a young man who had been seriously rejected by his own family. When he grew up he fell in love with a beautiful young lady and they were married. He finally had someone who loved him. Then he became tormented lest he would in some way lose the one who loved him. He felt compelled to smother his wife with protection. When he was at work he would call home to be sure that she was still there. He was haunted by fears that she might become unfaithful.

One day this man called home, and his wife did not answer the phone. When he arrived home that evening he confronted her. "Where were you this morning? I called at exactly ten twenty-three, and you did not answer the phone. Where did you go? Who were you with?" The young wife was already familiar with his pattern of suspicion, and she had a good, honest answer. She had merely gone to the grocery store to buy a can of beans for dinner. "Oh, yeah?" He replied. "Then let me see what you bought. Show me the receipt for the beans." This young husband's jealousy caused him to control and possess his wife. Such jealous domination of one spouse over another is nothing short of witchcraft, and it will either make a marriage miserable or else destroy it.

Some people lose friends as quickly as they gain them simply because they try to control their friends. The relationship is guarded by suspicion and possessiveness. The controlling person will not allow his friend to be anyone else's friend. In order to keep the friend from having any opportunity to relate to others, that friend must remain under surveillance twenty four hours a day. Who would feel comfortable with such continuous watchfulness? The easiest way out of the vise is to break the relationship. The result is rejection, the very thing that was being guarded against.

Rejection begets rejection. The rejected person becomes abnormal in his behavior, and others who try to have a relationship with such a person soon feel threatened and pressured. When the one placed under control decides to end the relationship, the other person is rejected. As strange as it is, the very thing the rejected person feared and was seeking to prevent resulted in another rejection. Like Job, the thing he feared came upon him.

Summary

The preceding examples of readjustments to the hurts of rejection represent common efforts to either alleviate the hurt or to find new ways to satisfy the love need in one's life. As each effort is examined, it is found to be either false or evil. These methods are not of God but are of the Evil One. Instead of escaping from problems, the problems are worsened.

As I have taught this message in deliverance seminars, there are some who have felt devastated by the time I reached this point in the teaching. Many persons have told me, "I have done everything wrong. You have described me on every point. I suppose there is no hope for me." Wait! There is hope. We are coming to that. First, we see the problem, and then we receive the answer. Bear with me until we examine one additional area of complication, and then we will come to the remedy.

V

Repercussions From Wrong Reactions and Wrong Readjustments

Wrong reactions and wrong readjustments to the hurts of rejection make bad matters worse. God's Word reminds us of the Divine law of sowing and reaping. "Whatsoever a man soweth, that shall he also reap" (Galatians 6:7). This is why we must learn to handle our hurts scripturally. Jesus was despised and rejected of men; yet, Jesus did not end up with a disintegrated personality, and neither was He demonized. Why? He handled his problems as the Father taught Him. When we walk in His steps, we will obtain the same results. When we handle our hurts wrongly, there will be repercussions.

WITHIN ONESELF

Imprisoned In Self

A professor once said, "A person wrapped up in himself makes a very small package." This is true, but, it is also true that a person wrapped up in himself is in a very strong prison. One becomes locked up in "self" by concentrating upon his hurts and their consequences.

The man or woman who dwells on all the negative things that have happened to him will soon become obsessed with "me," "myself" and "I." Everyone he meets will become an audience for his tale of woes. In what sense is this person in bondage? God has called us to love and serve others. A man imprisoned in himself is unable to give himself to others. He is not free to do what God has called him to do.

After prolonged concentration upon one's self and one's problems, a deep habit pattern is formed. One gets into a rut. He believes that he is incapable of helping others so long as his own troubles persist. He is rendered useless to the Kingdom of God, and Satan has gained the advantage.

Loss of Identity

If an individual, through self rejection, has taken on other personalities, he will manifest these various personalities from time to time. For example, those associated with him might find him withdrawn and insecure, and then right before their eyes he may become rebellious and vocal. The individual himself becomes confused about his own identity, and he begins to wonder "Who am I?" Such false personalities are demonic in composition—made up of systems of evil spirits. At times the individual's true personality emerges, and the nature of Jesus is seen. It is highly confusing for others to relate to someone who displays different personalities at different times. One wants to say, "Will the real person please stand up?"

There are also those who become extensions of someone else's personality and thereby lose their own identity and freedom. A son may become an extension of his father's life, whereupon the father programs his son to carry out the aims in life that he was unable to achieve for himself. Or, a mother may try to live out her unfulfilled love life through her daughter's marriage, thereby creating confusion, conflicts and jealousies. By yielding to a parent's control, the son or daughter is unable to fulfill God's calling. One must be free from parental domination if he is to develop into the person God wants him to become.

Entrapment

The problems of life can become so complicated that there appears to be no solution. When all hope of rescue is lost, one can easily become resigned to a life of defeat. He says to himself, "There is no way out of my plight. No one cares how much I hurt. God does not respond to my prayers." There is a demon named "Entrapment." He makes his sufferer feel as though he is in a rat maze. The hopelessness becomes so heavy that one ceases all efforts to extricate himself.

Withdrawal

There are varying methods and degrees of withdrawal. Withdrawal is escape from unpleasantness and responsibility. Persons who have been hurt tend to become adept at escape tactics. "Catatonia" is withdrawal taken to an extreme. Self is incapable of response. Life has become so unpleasant that permanent escape manifests itself in silence and immobility.

I once read the account of a compassionate man who began regular visits to a catatonic patient in a mental hospital. He would sit for hours and talk to the patient although there was no response in speech or countenance. This process went on for months. One day, as the two of them sat on the porch of the hospital ward, the friend saw a little squirrel on the lawn. He began to talk to the patient about the squirrel, and the patient responded. It was love that had broken the barrier. The patient from that point began to come out of his self-imposed prison.

A person withdraws because of rejection and fear of rejection. Relationships have proven painful, and the risk of more hurt is too great. When love is offered it cannot at first be received. It must be offered and proven over and over again. The Bible tells us that "love is patient." Even when his love is not accepted, a loving person keeps on pouring out more love. Patient love is necessary to bring some of the wounded out of their prisons. The deliverance counselor must be led by the Holy Spirit in weaving together the ministry of love and the ministry of deliverance. As demons are cast out with stern commands, the counselee must be loved and encouraged.

Cessation of Love

A person who has experienced a love trauma usually needs deliverance from a spirit of "fear of love." Love involvements can be deemed such failures that interest is lost in trying again. A representative illustration is the failure of love within a marriage. After a divorce there may be no interest in remarriage. The marriage was based on love, but love failed. The hurt was totally unexpected. The divorced person was put through a trauma. Who wants to go through that again? Why run the risk of another love failure? What guarantee is there against another hurt?

Abandonment Of Faith

Since "faith worketh by love," when love fails, faith fails (Galatians 5:6). In other words, when one loses confidence in God's love, he has no basis for faith. This is why God approaches us with His love rather than with His other attributes. God wants to evoke faith from us. Love draws faith from others. If you know someone loves you, then you can have faith in him.

When a man's faith fails, he stops depending upon God, and trys to work out his problems with his own resources. He is doomed to failure, for the Lord is his only answer. The man who loses trust in God loses the key to victory. No wonder the devil seeks to destroy our assurance of God's love, for thereby faith is ship-wrecked. Without faith it is impossible to please God or to receive anything from Him (see Hebrews 11:6; James 1:6-7).

Self-Deception

Self-deception is a false belief concerning self: one thinks he is right when he is wrong. Self-deception is a trap of the devil. It is extremely difficult for one to extricate himself from deception. When a person is deeply entangled in deception, a counselor is challenged to the maximum, for the deceived believes that he needs no help.

Self-deception is an outgrowth from rebellion and is rooted in rejection. The pattern is the same with all who are self-deceived. How, we may ask, does rejection result in self-deception? The one wounded by rejection must either respond with forgiveness or react in some sinful way. Often, the reaction to rejection is rebellion. Rebellion constitutes hatred, disrespect and dishonor which are expressed in disobedience. When a person becomes rebellious he refuses to yield to valid authority. Who then will provide oversight over his life? He becomes his own authority. He decides, "No authority will tell me what to do. I will do as I please."

Since rejection creates an emptiness in one's life, one seeks ways to fill important "hungers" within self, for he hungers for love, respect, honor, and fulfillment. Unless these needs are met in Christ, there is temptation to meet them in wrong ways. If he has rebelled against instruction and discipline, who can correct him? He has closed the door to correction and opened the door to self-deception.

The self deceived person has burned his bridges behind him. That is, he has become unanswerable to anyone, become his own authority and now refuses to accept any attempt from others to correct him.

A person will cling to a deception because it appears valuable. It seems to offer security, recognition, acceptance, approval or love. Since the deception seems so important, it is stoutly defended. When the deception is challenged, the person feels threatened. He becomes determined that no one will take away the one thing that makes him feel important or secure. Therefore, he had rather suffer persecution than give up his deception. Only by the grace of God will the seriously self-deceived person escape his bondage.

An outward manifestation of self-deception is a preoccupation with self. The deception becomes an obsession. It is foremost in the person's consciousness and conversation. There is an urgency to defend, strengthen, share and promote the deception.

Pride is a common companion to self-deception. Pride is the opposite of inferiority, and produces a counter balance to inferiority. Pride creates a false sense of superiority. When one has been belittled by others, he is prone to build himself up in his own estimation. Scripture warns against exalting oneself above measure.

For I say, through the grace given unto me, to every man that is among you. not to think of himself more highly than he ought to think; but to think soberly, according as God hath dealt to every man the measure of faith. Romans 12:3

Pride compounds rebellion and keeps a person from seeking or accepting needed counsel. When pride and unteachableness join forces with self-deception, a person is snared in serious bondage. How will he ever escape his deception? Although he has a completely false view of himself, he is blind to his own problem.

Self-deception is sometimes compounded by self-delusion. The Greek word for delusion is *plane* which means "a wandering, or going astray." The New Testament usage of this word always represents a mental straying, wrong opinion, or error in morals or religion. In Paul's second epistle to the Thessalonians, reference is made to the "man of sin...whose coming is after the working of Satan...with all deceivableness of unrighteousness in them that perish; because **they receive not the love of the truth, that they might be saved. And for this cause God shall send them strong delusion, that they should believe a lie"** (II Thessalonians 2:2, 9-11) (emphasis added).

When a lie replaces truth in a person's mind, the lie becomes fixed misconception. The delusion is clung to so strongly that all illumination is occluded. Until the deluded soul admits that he has embraced a lie and sets his will against it, further counsel is rendered useless. The following illustrations pinpoint types of delusions we have encountered.

A common delusion pertains to love and marriage. I know a woman who has believed for years that she will marry a certain young man, although the man has never shown any interest in her. She is convinced that God has revealed His will in the matter, and that the fellow will eventually propose marriage. Therefore, she refuses to date other eligible men and continually puts herself in his awareness through phone calls. Even though the man has moved to another city, she has not relaxed her belief that he will eventually fall in love with her. Her pastor and several of her closest friends have told her that she is deluded, yet she clings to the "lie." Unless she chooses to accept the truth, she is likely to die an old maid.

Divorce is a terrible tragedy which is sometimes compounded by a delusion which clings to a false hope. There are situations where divorce has taken place, the former spouse has remarried, and the person believes their former marriage will be restored. God does not sanction remarriage under these conditions. The hope is false.

> If a man put away his wife, and she go from him, and become another man's, shall he return to her again? shall not that land be greatly polluted? Jeremiah 3:1

Some are deluded as to power. We have ministered to persons who actually thought they were God. One man interrupted a service while I was teaching by shouting out, "I am God!" Of course, everyone present realized that he was deluded.

Another man rejoiced with us following his deliverance from demon spirits. He had actually believed that he had special mental powers which would enable him to detonate atomic bombs.

Other delusions pertain to belief that one is of special importance. We have encountered men who thought they were Moses, Elijah and Jesus. A man with a very unstable personality told us that he was once a child evangelist. He said that when he was abandoned by his parents, a minister and his wife adopted him. He insisted that at the age of four he went to Russia, Africa and Cuba to preach the Gospel. He told us that all the gifts of the spirit were in operation in his ministry and that thousands were saved and healed. He clung to this "lie," believing that one day he would be restored to his former place of spiritual ability and honor.

Even a deep understanding of the Word of God does not insure a man against becoming self-deluded, for he must not only know the truth, but he must love the truth! How many of us know ministers of the Gospel who have gone astray morally? How could one who knows the Word of God and who has preached it for years, fall into immorality? He has chosen to believe Satan's lies. Satan tells him that his love needs are not being fulfilled, whereupon he begins to fantasize illicit love affairs. As his mind becomes more and more deluded, he rationalizes away former convictions and believes himself an exception to God's holy commandments. When the opportunity for fornication or adultery arises, it is a short step between what he agrees with in his mind and what he commits with his body.

Another augmentation of self-deception is self-seduction. A man may be seduced by another person, but he can also seduce himself. That is, he may willfully choose to follow moral or doctrinal error. The process of self-seduction is usually a gradual one, as one "toys" with temptations.

> But every man is tempted, when he is drawn away of his own lust, and enticed. Then when lust hath conceived, it bringeth forth sin, and sin, when it is finished, bringeth for death. James 1:14,15

Each person has legitimate needs—spiritual, emotional and physical. God has provided ways for these needs to be met. For example, God has ordained that sexual needs be fulfilled within marriage. The needs of the stomach are to be satisfied with proper food eaten temperately. Sin's temptation is that we go outside of and in excess of God's imposed limitations. Lust is "over desire" in meeting proper needs.

In the wilderness temptations, Satan's approach to Jesus was based on legitimate needs. Jesus was hungry and needed bread. He was the Messiah and needed to establish His lordship. He was King of Kings and needed to establish His rule upon earth. Satan tempted Jesus to satisfy these needs in unlawful ways (see Matthew 4:1-11).

In Proverbs, chapter seven, is found the account of a young man's encounter with a prostitute. At first glance, it appears as though she seduced him. A closer study reveals a clear cut case of self-seduction. He flirted with temptation. He was not trying to avoid sin. He became "drawn away of his own lust, and enticed" (James 3:14).

> And behold among the simple ones. I discerned among the youths, a young man void of understanding, Passing through the street near her corner; and he went to her house. Proverbs 7:7,8

A young man of my acquaintance was bound by

drugs, alcohol and fornication. After months of intense teaching, counsel and deliverance he was set free. The Lord provided him with a good job. His fellow Christians loved him, and his future looked bright. In the midst of his victory he announced to his pastor his decision to go back into the ways of the world and take up his old life of sin. No one else had influenced him. He, too, was "drawn away of his own lust and enticed" James 1:14. His spiritual plight is pictured in the Word of God:

> For if after they have escaped the pollutions of the world through the knowledge of the Lord and Saviour Jesus Christ, they are again entangled therein, and overcome, the latter end is worse with them than the beginning. For it had been better for them not to have known the way of righteousness, than, after they have known it, to turn from the holy commandment delivered unto them. But it is happened unto them according to the true proverb, The dog is turned to his own vomit again; and the sow that was washed to her wallow in the mire. II Peter 2:20-22

The deceived will eventually become a deceiver, leading others into error. Jude calls the deceiver a "wandering star" (Jude 13). The Greek word translated "wandering star" is *planetes* from which our English word "planet" is derived. *Planetes* is a form of the word *plane*, the common Greek verb for "deceive." Thus, a self-deceived person is one who, like a star fallen out of orbit, has wandered off the course of truth. He is not only headed for self-destruction but also endangers others.

There is One who is never deceived, and Who knows the deceitful hearts of men. "The deceived and the deceiver are His [and in His power]" (Job 12:16, Amplified). Deception does not excuse one from the judgement of God.

Among Christians I have found four common

categories of self-deception:

First, there are those who are deceived in matters of Divine guidance. Believers need guidance; they need to hear God's voice. It is the spiritually minded man, who is intent upon receiving divine guidance, who is vulnerable to the false. The man of the world, who is disinterested in spiritual things, is not a target for false guidance.

I am reminded of a man who was raised in a traditional, denominational church. One day he had a deep spiritual experience in which he heard God speak through prophecy and also speak directly to his own spirit. He had a deep longing for a close walk with God. He wanted very much for God to continue speaking to him concerning every detail of life. He literally expected God to tell him what color of socks to put on each morning. On his way home from work he expected God to direct him at every intersection in the highway. Should he turn right or left or go straight ahead? Consequently, he began to "hear" what he thought was God speaking, but he was grossly deceived. The deception was made obvious by the resulting confusion. "God is not the author of confusion" (I Corinthians 14:33). He became so confused that he could not discern when God actually spoke. He could not be sure if he was hearing God, or the devil or his vain imagination. When God actually spoke, he could not be sure that it was God. When God had not spoken, he was following a lie.

"But what if it were God?" he questioned. A fear that he would fail God locked him into the deception. His fear of God was not "clean" (see Psalm 19:9). He feared God's condemnation. He was "not made perfect in love" (I John 4:18).

Many believers expect God to speak to their minds. God is a spirit being, and he communicates with man's spirit (see John 4:24). Until a believer understands how God speaks and learns to listen with spiritual ears, he is likely to experience much false guidance.

Some guidance-hungry Christians have made spiritual Ouija Boards out of their Bibles in an effort to hear from God. This mechanical method of seeking Divine guidance has been labeled, "flippin' the Good Book." The person seeking guidance will frame a question that he wants God to answer. Then, he will close his eyes, open his Bible at random, place a finger on the page and expect the verse his finger rests upon to be the answer to the question which he has asked God.

My wife and I were leading a series of deliverance services. A certain woman arrived early and took her seat in the church. When the pastor saw this woman he whispered to us that he was elated to see her in the meeting because she needed deliverance badly. He shared with us that this woman continually sought guidance by "flippin' the Good Book." I cautioned the pastor not to rejoice prematurely. I knew the devil did not want this woman in a deliverance meeting. Sure enough, before the service started the woman got up and walked out. The next day I met this woman on the street, and I asked her why she had left the service. She said that she had opened her Bible at random, and the Lord gave her scripture that told her she did not need deliverance and that she was to leave.

Rather frequently I find Christians who are guided by "voices." Most of these voices are counterfeits of God's audible speaking. These voices are heard in the mind rather than in the spirit. Sometimes the voices are audible. I have named these false guidance demons "Many Voices." Some individuals hear more than one voice.

Since demons are deceivers, they will usually begin by speaking things that sound fairly reasonable. When a person accepts the voice(s) as valid, then demons become very bold and lead the person into deep deception.

From time to time the news media carries reports of murders and other serious crimes committed by persons who were acting in obedience to a voice they thought was God. God does not speak contrary to His revealed Word, the Bible.

The Christian who is found to be led by false voices should be firmly counseled to lay aside all "voices" as a way of receiving guidance. He should ask God to provide guidance in other ways. As a safeguard against further deception, whatever guidance he claims to have received should be judged by those in spiritual authority over him.

Second, there are those who are deceived in matters of ministries and revelations. Each of us need to be needed. If one has never really felt important within his own family, he has an unfulfilled need to be of value to others. He is open to the deception that God has called him into a special ministry. Some of the most unstable people that I have met are convinced that God has, or is about to, thrust them into ministry.

A lady called my wife and me for counsel. She wanted to know how to go about getting rid of her husband and her children so that she could begin her ministry in the Lord. She said that one day she was washing dishes and the Lord revealed to her that He was thrusting her into a miracle healing ministry. As she lifted her hands to praise the Lord, there was heat in her hands. She thought this was the anointing. She failed to realize that she had just taken her hands out of hot dishwater!

She began picturing herself in a healing ministry. In her imagination she saw herself as another Katherine Kuhlman, moving gracefully on the platform of a huge auditorium with thousands of people being "slain in the spirit" and healed. She was anxious for her husband to come home from work so she could share the revelation of her calling with him. She met him at the door with, "God told me today that I am to have a great healing ministry like that of Katherine Kuhlman." The husband gave no response to her excitement. He wanted to know, "What's for dinner?"

The woman was crushed and angry. How could she have a healing ministry as long as she was married to a spiritually insensitive husband? Besides, she had three small children to look after. She would not have time to cook, wash and iron or run car pools. This is why she had called us for counsel. How could she get rid of her husband and children so that she could go into "her ministry."

A counselor must never agree with a person's deception. He must speak the truth in love. When we told her that she was deceived, she was offended. How did we know that God had not spoken to her? We explained that she already had a ministry. "What on earth might it be"? she asked. We explained that God had called her to the ministry of wife and mother, and that this is one of the most important ministries that a woman can have.

"What if it were God?" she questioned. "If I do not do what God has called me to do, then I will fail God." She asked the very question that holds so many in their deceptions, "But what if it were God?" Such supposed revelations must be tested by the Word of God. God's Word does not counsel wives to divorce their husbands or abandon their children in order to fulfill a ministry in the church.

God provides spiritual leaders to protect us from deception. When the lady called us she did not ask us to judge her revelation but to help her carry out her deception. Nevertheless, we were able to give counsel, and ultimately she agreed with the truth. We knew that we had saved her and her family from much heartache.

> *Obey your spiritual leaders and submit to them - continually recognizing their authority over you; for they are constantly keeping watch over your souls and guarding your spiritual welfare, as men who will have to render an account [of their trust]. [Do your part to] let them do this with gladness, and not with sighing and groaning, for that would not be profitable to you [either].* Hebrews 13:17, Amplified.

Third, there are those who are doctrinally deceived. Strange and "far out" doctrines are especially inviting to persons who are starved for love and acceptance, because they have a yearning to be uniquely important in the body of Christ. People who embrace false doctrines face many strong challenges which they consider persecutions. Deception causes them to believe that God is especially proud of them for standing their ground. They become convinced that they would fail God if they ever ceased to defend and promote their doctrine. Consequently, adherents to false doctrines are often more zealous than those who hold to true doctrines.

A man came to me for deliverance, but first he wanted to share a special doctrine that he had embraced. With great excitement he explained that he would never die physically. He had come into a special revelation that excluded him from death. He declared that whenever he passed a funeral parlor he would confess, "You will never get me!" He was completely obsessed with this "no death" doctrine.

Finally, the man got around to explaining why he thought he needed deliverance. He had fallen into deep depression, and at times he contemplated suicide. It amazed me that he had not seen the inconsistency between believing that he would never die and the fear that he would kill himself.

Fourth, there are those who are deceived about honor and position in life. They have an unfulfilled need to be respected. Most of these persons have been severely rejected and abused in childhood. Their deception is believing that they are destined to become renowned persons whom others will be forced to recognize.

A striking example of this deception of believing that one will become very prominent was the case of a teenaged boy who was brought to me by leaders in a Christian youth camp. The young man was convinced that he was destined to become the ruler or the entire world. He brought with him a very large notebook filled with his plans for world conquest. In the front there was a map of the world which showed the location of his planned world headquarters. There were designs for secret missile systems and related war equipment which would enable him to conquer the world. The notebook was very neatly done, and the information was in coded language which the young man interpreted. He was convinced that he was destined to become the supreme authority over all nations.

When the youth finished his explanation, I asked him one question: "What is your relationship with your father?" He hung his head and replied, "My father doesn't love me." "But if you became the ruler of the world, even your father would be forced to recognize your importance, Is that not true?" I asked. "Yes", he responded. Then, I went on to explain to him that his whole scheme of world conquest was a deception, and that all he was looking for was a father's love. It took much persuasive reasoning to convince him that he was grossly deceived, but eventually he agreed with the truth and was delivered.

The happy sequel to the story is that the father recognized his own failures and began to provide the loving relationship that his son so desperately needed. Several months later the two of them wrote me a letter to let me know of the victory they had gained.

Infirmities of Mind, Emotions and Body

Years ago I began to have severe chest pains. I was admitted to the hospital for tests. The doctor asked me if I had been under any pressures. I told him "no," but I was lying. I was embarrassed to admit that a few weeks earlier I had been dismissed from my position with my denomination because I had experienced the baptism in the Holy Spirit. My dismissal meant that I had lost my salary, my health insurance and my retirement program. My pride was wounded, and my closest friends now rejected me. I reacted with both resentment and fear. Next, a medical doctor was telling me that I had a heart problem.

The devil lost no time in taking advantage of my sinful reactions to rejection. After I repented and decided to trust God, the demons were cast out, and the heart infirmity ceased.

If we allow hurts to produce sinful reactions, sin will produce pressures, and pressures will produce infirmities. Many physical healings result from a thorough cleansing of one's life from sin and guilt, and the resulting demonization. The healing of the inner man is also the result of deliverance from demons which came into a person from wounds of rejection and from his sinful reactions and readjustments to the hurts.

FROM OTHERS

More Rejection

There is a direct relationship between inner hurts and an unstable personality. As we have seen, the fear of rejection causes a person to become distrustful and suspicious of others. His reaction to fear of further rejection has made him paranoid. His instability creates a discomfort in others who are trying to relate to him. So, others reject him. **Thus, rejection sets the stage for more rejection.** Life becomes a merry-go-round of hurt, reaction, rejection—and it is anything but merry.

Anyone seething with suspicion is like a pressure cooker building up steam. In the same way that a pressure cooker lets off steam through a safety valve when the pressure builds up to a danger point, a paranoid individual must also let off steam through confrontations. He lashes out and accuses those around him because he thinks they are working against him. His senseless confrontations offend others who, in turn, often retaliate with more hurts of rejection.

The unstable personality is characterized by unstable behavior. When the self-rejected takes on an alter ego, he becomes a puzzle to others. Which personality will emerge next? Will he be inwardly withdrawn and depressed, or will he be outwardly rebellious and angry? Such irregular behavioral patterns makes others uneasy, and rejection once again occurs.

When one loves another individual, and there is no recognition or reciprocation of that love, discouragement builds up quickly, Love invested in another's life is like money invested in a bank. If there is no return on the investment, one will move his deposit somewhere else.

Complicated personalities present a challenge. Optimistic helpers will accept the challenge. Alas, more is needed than zeal in order to untangle the complications. The unskilled counselor will eventually become frustrated and drop the project. Hopes of recovery are dashed, and the wounded soul is again wounded by fresh rejection.

Attracts Wrong Helpers

When the blind lead the blind, they both fall into the ditch. Those who are hurting are prone to share their problems with everyone who comes along. When problems are laid bare, the one who receives the report is placed in a position to respond. In other words, he is asked to become a counselor. As the list of unqualified counselors grows, more and more confusion is administered.

Too, there is no shortage of self-appointed helpers who falsely believe it is their calling from God to counsel everyone in sight. They have "a zeal, but not according to knowledge."

Again, there are many sympathizers. The wounded need more than sympathy. If the rejected one has already fallen into self pity, commiseration makes it worse.

Evokes Wrong Treatment

Wounds in the flesh are sensitive. They cannot be touched without pain. The same is true of inward wounds. Suppose a wife has suffered greatly in life and has a very low tolerance for abusiveness, and her husband does not know how to be gentle, kind and compassionate. He yells at his wife, "Why don't you shape up? You need to get hold of yourself. All that crying is driving me nuts. I'm going to call the authorities and have them put you in the crazy house." This wife's hurts are compounded by a heartless husband. She needs help desperately, and all she gets are **dogmatic demands without practical assistance.**

When one's problems are the result of rejection, any help offered must be wrapped in love. Even then, genuine help may be declined or deferred until the proffered love has been tested.

VI

Remedy for Rejection

Therefore all they that devour thee shall be devoured; and all thine adversaries, every one of them, shall go into captivity; and they that spoil thee shall be a spoil, and all that prey upon thee will I give for a prey. For I will restore health unto thee, and I will heal thee of thy wounds, saith the Lord because they called thee an Outcast, saying. This is Zion, whom no man seeketh after. Jeremiah 30:16-17

Our God has given an absolute promise of deliverance and healing. It is time for the oppressed to come to the Lord in faith. Jesus said, "He hath sent me to heal the brokenhearted, to preach deliverance to the captives...to set at liberty them that are bruised" Luke 4:18.

The Great Physician has laid down certain conditions for healing and deliverance. These requirements for restoration are simple, yet necessary.

Be Teachable

The first condition for restoration is teachableness. There are many changes required. Old ways of reacting and readjusting must be changed. Bad habit patterns of attitude and behavior must be reversed. Everything in one's life that is not Christlike must be brought up to that standard.

Pastors and counselors are spiritual doctors.

The "patient" submits his case for diagnosis and treatment. The "doctor" seeks wisdom and understanding from above. He prescribes what is needed to restore the "patient" to wholeness. Sometimes the "doctor's" diagnosis and treatment plan does not coincide with the "patient's" preconceived opinion and is refused by the "patient." This ties the "doctor's" hands, and he is unable to be of any help.

The average person cannot accurately diagnose his own ailments. He is prone to see the surface problems rather than the root problems. When he goes to a counselor for ministry, he must submit to his counselor and cooperate in what he is instructed to do.

Correction is not rejection! There have been many cases where I could not help those who came to me. Every legitimate change that I required of them seemed to them as punishment. This correction/rejection syndrome renders a person unteachable. Teachableness is within a person's will. He must agree to comply with the counsel given. He will accomplish nothing by running from counselor to counselor trying to find one who will agree with what he thinks. He must humbly admit, "The problem is in me. I must change."

Now no chastening for the present seemeth to be joyous, but grievous: nevertheless afterward it yieldeth the peaceable fruit of righteousness unto them which are exercised thereby. Hebrews 12:11

Forgive

Forgiveness of all who have offended is an absolute condition for deliverance. Forgiveness is a debt we owe which must never be allowed to relapse. "Owe no man any thing, but to love one another" (Romans 13:8). The instant forgiveness stops, unforgiveness begins. Anyone who expects God's forgiveness must forgive others.

Jesus told of a servant who owed a vast debt but had no means of making payment. The servant bowed down and asked his master to be patient. The lord of that servant was moved with compassion and forgave him the debt. This account pictures our sin indebtedness before God. There is no possibility that we can pay our sin debt, but when we ask the Lord for mercy, we are forgiven.

The servant who was forgiven his vast debt afterward refused to forgive a fellow servant a very small debt.

> *And his lord was wroth and delivered him to the tormentors, till he should pay all that was due unto him.* Matthew 18:34

Christ's next statement applies to us:

> *So likewise shall my heavenly Father do also unto you, if ye from your hearts forgive not every one his brother their trespasses.* Matthew 18:35

What does the heavenly Father do to us when we fail to forgive others? **He turns us over to the tormentors!** Demon spirits are the tormentors.

It is a very serious matter not to forgive others their trespasses. A man's forgiveness from God is revoked when he refuses to forgive others. Unforgiveness places one under a curse, and demon spirits are permitted to torment him.

Forgiveness is not a feeling; it is a rational decision, an act of the will. Our act of forgiving is compliance with God's command. God says that if we expect His forgiveness, we must be forgiving. If we choose not to forgive, we can expect to be tormented until we do. When God has turned a man over to demons no deliverance minister on earth can get him out of prison until he meets God's conditions. The resulting torment may be manifested in his life through his mind, emotions, physical body or life circumstances.

Forgiveness must also be extended to oneself. After God's forgiveness has been accepted, one must forgive himself. The Accuser will say, "You do not deserve to be forgiven. What you did is inexcusable. You must carry the shame and guilt of your sin the rest of your life." Unforgiveness toward self can lock a person into bondage just as surely as will his unforgiveness toward others.

Forget

Past hurts must be forgotten. The demon of "memory recall" must be cast out, for there is a demon whose expertise is to keep alive the memory of past wrongs. It is as though this fiend has a library of cassette tapes with detailed recordings of all the hurtful events in one's life which he plays over and over in the mind of his victim. The demon uses these memory stimulators to keep vividly alive painful memories of past hurts. The continual remembrance of past offenses keeps alive unforgiveness, bitterness and hatred.

The Apostle Paul spoke of his determination to forget whose things which are behind [the past] (see Philippians 3:13, amplification added). This principle of forgetting should be forcefully applied to the record of past trespasses against us. By remembering unpleasant and hurtful events of the past, the present is also ruined and each successive day is spoiled. Such remembrances serve no useful purpose. **So, we must remember to forget.**

Repent

It is altogether possible that one's own misconduct is the seedbed for hurts ministered by others. God requires complete honesty and humility as we come before His throne.

> Search me, O God, and know my heart, try me, and know my thoughts: And see if there be any wicked way in me, and lead me in the way everlasting. Psalm 139:23,24

Hurts experienced are usually more obvious than hurts administered. It is easier to recognize sin in another's life than in one's own. **How many times have we rejected others and caused them sorrow?** All sin calls for repentance. The only way to receive God's forgiveness is to enter into His presence through the door of repentance.

It is altogether possible that wrong reactions and wrong readjustments to hurts have not been seen as actual sins. **All deviation from the revealed will of God is sin.** Negative reactions and readjustments to suffered wrongs are contrary to God's commands and to His counsel. Additional sin doors are opened which permit additional demons to enter. Repentance of sin causes demons to know that their door of entrance has been found out. Repentance is the prelude to deliverance. **There can be no deliverance apart from genuine repentance.**

Be Reconciled

Reconciliation is the restoration of a broken relationship. Through the Cross God achieved reconciliation of sinners. For God "hath reconciled us to himself by Jesus Christ" (II Corinthians

77

5:18). The Greek word "reconciliation" denotes a complete change, a change from enmity to friendship. It is in this same context concerning reconciliation that God declares,

> *Therefore if any man be in Christ, he is a new creature; old things are passed away; behold, all things are become new.* II Corinthians 5:17

The shed blood of Jesus makes possible a complete change in things, and that change is reconciliation. Through reconciliation, those who were once God's enemies become His children and partakers of His divine nature.

Was it not sufficient that God simply forgive us? No, God desired more than a collection of forgiven sinners. He wanted a restored relationship with sinful man. When Adam and Eve sinned, the transgression passed down to all of us, and fellowship with God was destroyed. Through reconciliation our fellowship with God has been restored (See: Romans 5:17-19).

Is it not sufficient that we simply forgive others? No, God desires restored relationships. Forgiveness of others is the prelude to reconciliation. Reconciliation is a two-sided affair. It must be offered on the part of one and must be accepted on the part of the other. This is the way our reconciliation with God is achieved. God offers it, but we must accept it. The process of reconciliation is accomplished between two persons when the restoration of relationship is initiated by one person and accepted by the other.

We cannot force others to be reconciled to us, but God has made it plain that we must never let any failure to achieve reconciliation rest at our feet. "If it be possible, as much as lieth in you, live peaceably with all men" (Romans 12:18).

It can be unsettling, to say the least, to contemplate a restored relationship with those who have caused deep wounds. It should be kept in mind that the true test of successful reconciliation is the issuance of peace. If a restored relationship is peaceable, free from strife and disorder, then it is not feared but enjoyed.

Stabilize In God's Love

Jesus was "despised and rejected of men" yet He did not suffer from a disturbed personality (Isaiah 53:3). There is one basic reason why Jesus remained stable though wounded: He was secure in the Father's love. He could yield to the Father's will, even unto death on the Cross, because He knew the Father loved Him. He could bear the terrible rejection of men because He was anchored in the Father's love.

> *The Father loveth the Son, and hath given all things into his hand John 3:35. The Father loveth the Son, and sheweth him all things that himself doeth John 5:20.*

It is the faithfulness of God the Father's love, rather than the faithfulness of human love, which provides security and strength to rebound from hurts and wounds. It is a common mistake to assume that when human love has failed, God's love has also failed. Jesus gave the following words of assurance so we, too, can remain stable in spite of the adversities suffered at the hands of others. "The Father himself loveth you" John 16:27.

Rejection hurt has the same effect upon a person's trust in love that a broken railroad track has upon a train—derailment! How can one come to trust in love again? There can never be a full guarantee that any human love will not fail or disappoint. There is only one love that is incapable of failure—God's love. Therefore, trust in God's love creates stability in the inner man.

Stabilize In Human Love

Trust in God's love is a foundation providing courage to risk human relationships based on love. I say, "risk" because it is a fact that all human love is capable of failure. However, the more one is surrounded with stable human love, the easier it is for him to overcome the repercussions of rejection's lacerations.

In emphasizing how the members of the body of Christ should minister to one another, Paul wrote, "Let love be without dissimulation (pretence or hypocrisy)" Romans 12:9, amplification added. There are so many persons who have been rejected by their own families. They are starved for love. The church, the family of God, should provide a healing climate for those robbed of love in other areas of life.

How can one know when he is stabilized in love? **First**, he is able to pour out his love upon others without demanding reciprocation. He can love without being loved. **Second**, he can meet recurrences of rejection with forgiveness. He will not react wrongly by anger, resentment or self-pity.

Be Delivered

Deliverance is salvation. The Greek word "soteria" denotes deliverance, preservation and salvation. This word encompasses all the blessings bestowed by God on men in Christ through the Holy Spirit. Deliverance from evil spirits is a provi-

80

sion of the Cross, Jesus defeated Satan, destroyed the works of the devil, and gave His followers power over all the power of the enemy.

Deliverance is appropriated by believers when they confront demon spirits with God given authority. The remedy for demonization is the casting out of the oppressing, troubling, tormenting, controlling and hindering spirits.

By the time a person has read the preceding material in this book, he should have a clear picture of his need for deliverance. It is rare to find a person who does not require a degree of deliverance from evil spirits which gained entrance through the consequences of rejection.

Deliverance is the way to inner healing. Christ provided it for this very purpose. Evil spirits are responsible for most instability in the personality, and inner healing is experienced as demons are driven out. A believer may be able to minister deliverance to himself, but initially it is best if he can be prayed for by a qualified deliverance counselor.[1]

Fill the House

When the unclean spirit is gone out of a man, he walketh through dry places, seeking rest, and findeth none. Then he findeth it empty, swept, and garnished Then goeth he, and taketh with himself seven other spirits more wicked than himself; and they enter in and dwell there: and the last state of that man is worse than the first. Matthew 12:43-45

It is one thing to cast out demons and another thing to keep them out. Some have found the maintenance of deliverance more difficult than the

---

[1]See *PIGS IN THE PARLOR*, A Practical Guide To Deliverance, by Frank and Ida Mae Hammond. Impact Books, Inc.

actual deliverance. If the demons cast out are not kept out, can it be truthfully said that deliverance has taken place?

Jesus emphasized the importance of maintaining deliverance when he used the analogy of filling a house which had been made vacant by the eviction of previous tenants. Jesus taught that demons can, as opportunity affords, return to the one out of whom they were cast. No permanent victory is gained through merely exorcising indwelling demons.

Jesus also warned that unless demons are prevented from returning, they can return in greater force. The expelled demons see a life which is merely emptied of their presence as an opening to return with companion spirits more wicked than themselves.

The whole purpose of cleansing oneself from sin and demons is to be filled with His likeness. If one's aim is merely to be rid of bothersome problems, his objective is shortsighted.

Having therefore these promises, dearly beloved, let us cleanse ourselves from all filthiness of the flesh and spirit, perfecting holiness in the fear of God. II Corinthians 7:1

The key questions which arise are: Who does the filling? How is the filling accomplished? With what must one be filled?

The one who receives deliverance is responsible for filling his own house. There is no example in Scripture of Jesus filling anyone's house for him. Assistance can be given by others, but the burden rests on the newly delivered. No one can be spiritual in our behalf: we must be spiritual in and of ourselves.

A cleansed vessel must be filled with the opposite from which it was emptied. If fear was cast out, faith must be added. If corruption was cast out, purity must fill its place. If hatred and bitterness were cast out, love and forgiveness must occupy. In other words, one must fill himself with the character and nature of Christ Himself. When a man is completely occupied with matters of the Holy Spirit, **there can be no room for evil.** "Walk in the Spirit, and ye shall not fulfill the lust of the flesh" (Galatians 5:16).

The filling of the house is accomplished by living a disciplined Christian life.

> Let not sin therefore reign in your mortal body, that ye should obey it in the lusts thereof. Neither yield ye your members as instruments of unrighteousness unto sin: but yield yourselves unto God, as those that are alive from the dead, and your members as instruments of righteousness unto God. Romans 6:12,13

Receive God's Comfort

Deliverance deals with only part of the problem caused by rejection. Deliverance may be compared with the cleansing of infection from a wound. Infection complicates an existing wound. Indeed, infection prevents a wound from healing, but once the infection is eliminated the wound itself can be healed. This analogy enables us to understand why one more step is necessary in order to complete the healing of rejection's wounds. After the unclean spirit (the infection) has been removed, the initial wound can then be healed.

The wound of rejection causes sorrow. "By sorrow of heart the spirit is broken (wounded)" (Proverbs 15:13). The remedy for sorrow is comfort. "A voice was heard in Ramah, lamentation, and bitter weeping; Rachel weeping for her children refused to be comforted" (Jeremiah 31:15).

Where does comfort come from? Comfort comes from God. "Blessed be God...the God of all comfort; Who comforteth us in all our tribulation..." II Corinthians 1:3,4.

How is comfort obtained? It is received as a gift of God's grace. It is obtained in the same way as salvation from sin. "For by grace are ye saved through faith..." Ephesians 2:8. Jesus sent the Holy Spirit to administer what He had purchased for us on the Cross.

> And I will pray the Father, and he shall give you another Comforter, that he may abide with you for ever...I will not leave your comfortless: I will come to you. I John 14:16,18

Inner healing is received no differently than physical healing. One may ask in faith and be healed (see Matthew 9:22). Or, he may call for the elders of the church who will anoint him with oil and pray the prayer of faith (see James 5:14-16).

> Therefore I say unto you, What things soever ye desire, when ye pray, believe that ye receive them and ye shall have them. Mark 11:24

Today Jesus asks every rejection-wounded soul the same question he asked the wretched, lame man beside the pool of Bethesda, "Wilt thou be made whole?" John 5:6. Give your hurts to Jesus. Choose to be comforted.

"Sarah," the young woman suffering from schizophrenia, whose story is related in *Pigs In The Parlor*, tells her own amazing story in *OUT OF THE VALLEY OF DARKNESS.*

"Sarah" (actually Mary-Etta Hinkle) had a relatively normal life. She was loved, but somehow couldn't accept the love from her family. What were *the factors* and *contributing influences* that caused her to become schizophrenic, and what is more important, *how* was she set free?

You will learn for yourself as the real life "Sarah" lays her life open before you without whitewashing any of her problems.

(The following is from the PREFACE COMMENT by Frank Hammond...)

"...Over the years many people have inquired about "Sarah." They have asked, "How is she doing?" "Was she really delivered from schizophrenia?" "Has she kept her deliverance?"

... Tears of joy and thanksgiving flooded our eyes as we read the manuscript..."

OUT OF THE VALLEY OF DARKNESS $6.95

Available from
IMPACT BOOKS, INC. 137 W. Jefferson,
Kirkwood, MO 63122

CERDOS EN LA SALA

More than 500,000 copies of PIGS IN THE PARLOR, the recognized handbook of Deliverance, are continuing to help set people free around the world from demonic bondages. This Bestseller is now also available IN SPANISH — at the same price as the English edition.

Paperback 5.95

KINGDOM LIVING FOR THE FAMILY

A long awaited sequel to PIGS IN THE PARLOR, offering not mere unrealistic theories, but rather a Practical Plan for implementing divine order in the family, and preventing the need for deliverance.

Paperback 5.95

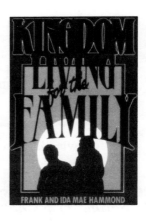

OVERCOMING REJECTION

Powerful help for confronting and dealing with rejection, which so often is found to be a root in individuals requiring deliverance. This book will help understand a tool commonly employed by the enemy in his attacks upon believers.

Paperback 3.95

THE SAINTS AT WAR

Too many Christian Soldiers are remaining inactive and ineffective in this hour of battle. This book is both a "call to arms" and an instruction manual to enable the Church, God's Army, to become aggressively militant toward its enemy, and that all the Saints of God might become SAINTS AT WAR.

Paperback 3.95

Booklets:

GOD WARNS AMERICA

In a night vision the author was shown three terrible judgments to come upon America: economic, bloodshed, and persecution of the Church. God reveals why and what must be done to avert the outpouring of His wrath.

Booklet 2.00

FAMILIAR SPIRITS

Brief, simple, but helpful scriptural information on this category of spirits and how to deal with them.

Booklet 2.00

SOUL TIES

Are a reality. Booklet explains what must be done to break them.

Booklet 2.00

Please send minimum postage of $1.50 plus 20¢ per book with your order.

FRANK HAMMOND
Author of PIGS IN THE PARLOR: amplifies and expands the teachings of this important book in several series of cassettes. In these tapes he reveals additional truths gleaned from his own far-reaching ministry in the area of deliverance and related fields. Much, much needed truth and light to be gained from his right insights and down-to-earth teaching. (3.95 each) **

DELIVERANCE SERIES:
_____ 1. HEALING THE PERSONALITY
_____ 2. THE SCHIZOPHRENIA REVELATION (I)
_____ 3. THE SCHIZOPHRENIA REVELATION (II)
_____ 4. MAINTAINING DELIVERANCE
_____ 5. DEALING WITH PRESSURES
_____ 6. THE ARM OF FLESH

FREEDOM FROM BONDAGE SERIES:
_____ 1. ESCAPE INTO BONDAGE
_____ 2. BONDAGE TO SIN
_____ 3. BONDAGE TO SELF
_____ 4. BONDAGE TO MAN
_____ 5. BREAKING OF CURSES
_____ 6. FLESH VS. SPIRIT

FAITH SERIES:
_____ 1. THINGS THAT DESTROY FAITH
_____ 2. THINGS THAT ENCOURAGE FAITH
_____ 3. THE LANGUAGE OF FAITH
_____ 4. CORRESPONDING ACTION OF FAITH
_____ 5. THE DEVELOPMENT OF FAITH
_____ 6. PRAYING THE PRAYERS OF PAUL

END-TIME SERIES:
_____ 1. END-TIME BEHAVIOR (PART I)
_____ 2. END-TIME BEHAVIOR (PART II)
_____ 3. END-TIME BEHAVIOR (PART III)
_____ 4. END-TIME BEHAVIOR (PART IV)
_____ 5. THE CHRISTIAN & TRIBULATION
_____ 6. THE UNRIGHTEOUSNESS & GOD'S

MESSAGES ON LOVE SERIES:
_____ 1. FRIENDSHIP
_____ 2. MY BROTHER'S KEEPER
_____ 3. THE PERFECTING LOVE
_____ 4. LEARNING TO LOVE
_____ 5. REMEMBERING TO FORGET

WALK IN THE SPIRIT SERIES:
_____ 1. FUNCTIONING AS SPIRITUAL MEN
_____ 2. SPIRITUAL PERCEPTION
_____ 3. SEEING INTO THE SPIRITUAL REALM
_____ 4. THE FRUIT OF RIGHTEOUSNESS
_____ 5. WHAT ADVANTAGE MY RIGHTEOUSNESS
_____ 6. THE MINISTRY OF EDIFICATION

SPIRITUAL MEAT SERIES:
_____ 1. THE LORD'S SUPPER
_____ 2. DISCERNING THE LORD'S BODY
_____ 3. WORSHIP & PRAISE
_____ 4. WHAT DEFILES A MAN
_____ 5. "STABILIZE"
_____ 6. KNOWING WHO YOU ARE AS A BELIEVER

FAMILY IN THE KINGDOM SERIES:
_____ 1. THE HUSBAND'S HEADSHIP
_____ 2. THE WIFE'S SUBMISSION
_____ 3. THE WIFE'S INFLUENCE
_____ 4. BRINGING UP CHILDREN (PART I)
_____ 5. BRINGING UP CHILDREN (PART II)
_____ 6. THE WIFE'S SANCTIFICATION (IDA MAE HAMMOND)

CHURCH SERIES:
_____ 1. THE BODY OF CHRIST
_____ 2. THE FAMILY OF GOD
_____ 3. THE TEMPLE OF GOD
_____ 4. GOD' HUSBANDRY
_____ 5. THE ARMY OF GOD
_____ 6. THE BRIDE OF CHRIST

RECOGNIZING GOD SERIES:
_____ 1. GOD OUR SOURCE
_____ 2. GOD OUR PROVIDER
_____ 3. GOD OUR REFUGE

★ ★ ★ ★ ★ ★ ★ ★ ★ ★ ★ ★ ★ ★ ★ SPECIAL OFFERS ★ ★ ★ ★ ★ ★ ★ ★ ★ ★ ★ ★ ★ ★ ★ ★

A) All 56 tapes listed above $170.00 (Save more than $50.00!)
B) Each 6 tape series Special Price only $19.75! (You pay for 5 tapes, 6th tape is FREE)
C) Buy any 12 tapes at $3.95 and you may choose 2 bonus tapes FREE of charge.

FOR THOSE SEEKING MORE INFORMATION..
...ABOUT DEMONOLOGY & DELIVERANCE

Banks, Bill
____MINISTERING TO ABORTION'S AFTERMATH ....P 5.95
____POWER FOR DELIVERANCE...P 5.95
____DELIVERANCE FOR CHILDREN..P 5.95
____DELIVERANCE FROM CHILDLESSNESS...............................P 5.95
____DELIVERANCE FROM FAT ....P 5.95

Basham, Don
____CAN A CHRISTIAN HAVE A DEMON? ....P 5.95
____DELIVER US FROM EVIL..P 9.00

Garrison, Mary
____BINDING & LOOSING...P 5.95
____HOW TO TRY A SPIRIT..P 5.95

Hagin, Kenneth
____ORIGIN & OPERATION OF DEMONS ....P 1.95
____DEMONS & HOW TO DEAL WITH THEM ....P 1.95
____MINISTERING TO THE OPPRESSED ....P 1.95
____BIBLE ANSWERS ABOUT DEMONS ....P 1.95

Hammond, Frank
____COMFORT FOR THE WOUNDED SPIRIT..............................P 3.95

_____DEMONS & DELIVERANCE...P 5.95
_____PIGS IN THE PARLOR ....P 5.95
_____KINGDOM LIVING FOR THE FAMILY ....P 5.95
_____OVERCOMING REJECTION ....P 3.95
_____SAINTS AT WAR..P 3.95
_____SOUL TIES (Booklet) ....P 2.00
_____FAMILIAR SPIRITS (Booklet)....................................P 2.00

Lindsay, Gordon
_____JOHN G. LAKE SERMONS ON DOMINION OVER
        DEMONS, DISEASE AND DEATH...............................P 4.95
_____SATAN'S REBELLION AND FALL...............................P 1.95
_____SATAN FALLEN ANGELS AND DEMON.....................P 1.95
_____SATAN'S DEMON MANIFESTATIONS........................P 2.95

Prince, Derek
_____EXPELLING DEMONS..P 1.25
_____SPIRITUAL WARFARE ....P 3.50
        SERIES ON DELIVERANCE - ON CASSETTE
_____6001 HOW I CAME TO GRIPS WITH DEMONS ....C 5.95
_____6002 HOW JESUS DEALT WITH DEMONS...............C 5.95
_____6003 NATURE AND ACTIVITY OF DEMONS ....C 5.95
_____6004 HOW TO RECOGNIZE & EXPELL DEMONS ....C 5.95
_____6005 CULT & OCCULT: SATAN'S SNARES ....C 5.95
_____6006 7 WAYS TO KEEP YOUR DELIVERANCE.........C 5.95
_____6007 TEENAGERS:YOUTH'S PLACE AND PROBLEMS
        IN THE END-TIMES ....C 5.95
_____6008 CHILDREN (5-11) INSTRUCTIONS ON
        DELIVERANCE FOR CHILDREN & PARENT ....C 5.95
_____SET OF 6001 - 6006 ..... SPECIAL 30.50
_____SET OF 6001 - 6008 ..... SPECIAL 40.50
        **SAVE $40.25 - Entire Set of Above Books & Tapes ONLY $122.00
        **SAVE $28.65 - Entire Set of Books (No Tapes) ONLY $86.00

...ABOUT THE ENEMY AND OUR ROLE

Alsobrook, David
_____THE ACCUSER ....P 3.00
Banks, William
_____POWER FOR DELIVERANCE.....................................P 5.95
_____THE HEAVENS DECLARE... ....P 6.95
Brant, Roxanne
_____HOW TO TEST PROP., PREACHING & GUIDANCE..............P 6.95
Hagin, Kenneth
_____THE BELIEVER'S AUTHORITY...................................P 3.95
White, Anne
_____TRIAL BY FIRE..P 3.50
        SAVE $4.55 - Entire Set of Books ONLY $25.75

...ABOUT THE BAPTISM OF THE HOLY SPIRIT

Banks, Bill
_____ALIVE AGAIN! ....P 4.95

Basham, Don
___HANDBOOK ON HOLY SPIRIT BAPTISM ....P 4.95
Delgado, Gabriele
___A LOVE STORY ....P 1.25
Gilles, George & Harriett
___SCRIPTURAL OUTLINE OF THE BAPTISM IN THE
    HOLY SPIRIT ....P 2.00
Hagin, Kenneth
___SEVEN VITAL STEPS TO RECEIVING THE H.S. ....P 1.95
Lindsay, Gordon
   SERIES ON GIFTS OF THE HOLY SPIRIT
___VOLUME 1 ....P 4.95
___VOLUME 2 ....P 4.95
___VOLUME 3 ....P 4.95
___VOLUME 4 ....P 4.95
Prince, Derek
___BAPTISM IN THE HOLY SPIRIT ....P 2.95
Sherrill, John
___THEY SPEAK WITH OTHER TONGUES ....P 6.95
Tari, Mel
___LIKE A MIGHTY WIND ....P 6.95
    SAVE $7.75 - Entire Set of Books ONLY $44.00

...ABOUT HEALING FROM GOD

Banks, Bill
___ALIVE AGAIN! ....P 4.95
___HOW I WAS HEALED OF CANCER & BAPTISED
    THE HOLY SPIRIT - (1 hr. cassette) ....C 3.95
___THREE KINDS OF FAITH FOR HEALING ....P 3.95
___DELIVERANCE FROM BARRENNESS ....P 5.95
Bosworth, F.F.
___CHRIST THE HEALER ....P 9.00
Hagin, Kenneth
___HEALING BELONGS TO US ....P 1.95
___KEYS TO SCRIPTURAL HEALING ....P 1.95
Lindsay, Gordon
   SERIES ON DIVINE HEALING & HEALTH
___CHRIST THE GREAT PHYSICIAN ....P 1.95
___HOW YOU CAN HAVE DIVINE HEALTH ....P 1.95
___BIBLE SECRET OF DIVINE HEALTH ....P 1.95
___HOW YOU CAN BE HEALED ....P 1.95
___REAL REASON WHY CHRISTIANS ARE SICK ....P 3.95
___30 BIBLE REASONS WHY CHRIST HEALS TODAY ....P 2.95
___25 OBJECTIONS TO DIVINE HEALING & ANS ....P 1.95
___WHY DO THE RIGHTEOUS SUFFER? ....P 1.95
___WHY SOME ARE NOT HEALED ....P 1.95
___DIFFICULT QUESTIONS ON DIVINE HEALING ....P 1.95
___...SET OF ABOVE SERIES (10 Titles) ....SET 19.00
MacMillen, S.I.
___NONE OF THESE DISEASES ....P 6.95
    SAVE $12.25 - Entire Set of Books ONLY $48.90

...ABOUT GROWING IN SPIRIT & FAITH

Banks, Bill
____ALIVE AGAIN! ....P 4.95
____THE HEAVENS DECLARE ....P 6.95
Brant, Roxanne
____MINISTERING TO THE LORD.....................................P 4.50
Buess, Bob
____FAVOR, THE ROAD TO SUCCESS ....P 2.50
Bush, Wes,
____HOW TO HEAR GOD SPEAK.....................................P 1.50
Carothers, Merlin
____POWER IN PRAISE..P 5.95
Hagin, Kenneth
____HOW TO TURN YOUR FAITH LOOSE ....P 1.95
____WHAT FAITH IS..P 1.95
Johnson, Gordon D.
____THE GLORIOUS CROSS OF ST. JOHN ....P 8.95
Jones, Russell B.
____GOLD FROM GOLGOTHA..P 1.50
Miller, Basil
____GEORGE MUELLER ....P 3.95
Trumbull, H.C.
____THE BLOOD COVENANT...P 8.95
Wigglesworth, Smith
____EVERINCREASING FAITH ....P 2.50
____FAITH THAT PREVAILS ....P 1.95
Whyte, Maxwell
____THE POWER OF THE BLOOD ....P 4.95

SAVE $9.45 - Entire Set of Books ONLY $53.50

- -

TOTAL QUANTITY _____ TOTAL ORDER   _____

Missouri Residents add 6% Sales Tax   _____

Minimum Postage $1.50 for one book:
PLUS .20 for each additional item   _____

TOTAL AMOUNT ENCLOSED   _____

Prices subject to change.
Write for complete catalog of over 600 Christian Books
IMPACT BOOKS, INC. 137 W. Jefferson, Kirkwood, MO 63122

THE HEAVENS DECLARE . . .
William D. Banks

More than 250 pages!
More than 50 illustrations!

- Who named the stars and why?
- What were the original names of the stars?
- What is the secret message hidden in the stars?

The surprising, **secret message** contained in the earliest, original names of the stars, is revealed in this new book.

The deciphering of the star names provides a fresh revelation from the heart of **the intelligence** behind creation. Ten years of research includes material from the British Museum dating prior to 2700 B.C.

A clear explanation is given showing that early man had a sophisticated knowledge of One, True God!

$6.95 + $1.00 Shipping/Handling

ALIVE AGAIN!
William D. Banks

The author, healed over twelve years ago, relates his own story. His own testimony presents a miracle or really a series of miracles — as seen through the eyes of a doubting skeptic, who himself becomes the object of the greatest miracle, because he is Alive Again!

The way this family pursues and finds divine healing as well as a great spiritual blessing provides a story that will at once bless you, refresh you, restore your faith or challenge it! You will not be the same after you have read this true account of the healing gospel of Jesus Christ, and how He is working in the world today.

The healing message contained in this book needs to be heard by every cancer patient, every seriously ill person, and by every Christian hungering for the reality of God.

More than a powerful testimony — here is teaching which can introduce you or those whom you love to healing and to a new life in the Spirit!

$4.95 + $1.00 Shipping/Handling

A BLOOD COVENANT IS THE MOST SOLEMN, BINDING AGREEMENT POSSIBLE BETWEEN TWO PARTIES.

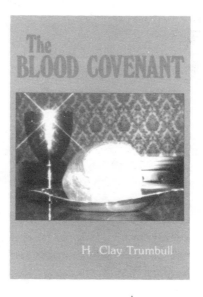

Perhaps one of the least understood, and yet most important and relevant factors necessary for an appreciation of the series of covenants and covenant relationships that our God has chosen to employ in His dealings with man, is the concept of the BLOOD COVENANT!

In this volume which has been "sold out," and "unavailable" for generations, lies truth which has blessed and will continue to bless every pastor, teacher, every serious Christian desiring to "go on with God."

Andrew Murray stated it beautifully years ago, when he said that if we were to but grasp the full knowledge of what God desires to do for us and understood the nature of His promises, it would "make the Covenant the very gate of heaven! May the Holy Spirit give us some vision of its glory."

$8.95

POWERFUL NEW BOOK
BY SAME AUTHOR . . .

This new book is unique because it offers real help for the suffering women who have already had abortions. This book is full of GOOD NEWS!

It shows how to minister to them, or may be used by the women themselves as it contains simple steps to self-ministry.

Millions of women **have had abortions**: every one of them is a potential candidate for the type of ministry presented in this book. Every minister, every counsellor, every Christian should be familiar with these truths which can set people free.

$5.95 + $1.00 Shipping/Handling

IMPACT BOOKS, INC.
137 W. Jefferson, Kirkwood, Mo. 63122

THREE KINDS OF FAITH FOR HEALING

Many today have been taught that the only way to be healed is to personally have faith for their healing. It is implied, one must somehow 'work up' or develop enough personal *faith-to-be-healed,* and then healing will come. Many have also been told that the reason they remain afflicted is because of their lack of faith.

Such statements in addition to being utterly devoid of compassion, are terribly devastating to the poor hearers. One could never imagine Jesus saying something so heartless. Yet these things are often said today. Even those who have not heard these words spoken aloud have received them through implication from proud, spiritually 'superior' friends who believe that these sick individuals are somehow deficient in faith.

There is good news both for them and for us, because that teaching is wrong. There are more ways of being healed than just the one way, as we have been taught.

In this new book, Bill Banks presents a *revelation* of three main types of faith for healing illustrated in Scripture, and a fourth which is a combination of the other three.

Three Kinds of Faith For Healing   Paper 3.95

FOR ADDITIONAL COPIES WRITE:

137 WEST JEFFERSON
KIRKWOOD, MISSOURI 63122

AVAILABLE AT YOUR LOCAL BOOKSTORE, OR YOU MAY
ORDER DIRECTLY. Toll-Free, order-line only M/C, DISC,
or VISA 1-800-451-2708.